For my mother, who has always been adventurous and ready to explore new experiences. She is even prepared to share this dedication with Cleopatra, my Siamese cat, who inspects my cooking from her perch on top of the fridge, and observes my writing at a safe distance from the noisy, unpredictable printer.

Copyright © 1990 Diane Seed

Illustration Copyright © 1990 Robert Budwig

First published in 1990 by The Ten Speed Press,
PO Box 7123, Berkeley, California 94707

Reprinted 1991

First published in Great Britain in 1990 by:
Rosendale Press Ltd, Premier House,
10 Greycoat Place, London SW1P 1SB

Designed by Robert Budwig
Typeset by Phoenix Photosetting, Chatham
Origination by Peak Litho Plates Ltd., Tunbridge Wells
Printed in Singapore by C.S. Graphics Pte Ltd.

Library of Congress Cataloging-in-Publication Data
Seed, Diane
Favorite Indian Food/Diane Seed: Illustrated by Robert Budwig
        p.          cm.
ISBN 0-89815-357-3
1. Cookery.    India.    I. Title
TX724.5.14S36     1990      90-31809
641.5954–dc20

FAVORITE

INDIAN

F·O·O·D

AUTHENTIC REGIONAL
RECIPES
by
DIANE SEED

ILLUSTRATED
BY
ROBERT BUDWIG

TEN·SPEED·PRESS

# Contents

Stuffed chicken breasts
Nine jewelled chicken
Chettinad chicken pepper fry
Cochin chicken with green chilli
Chicken cardamom

Pork with honey
Lamb with yoghurt and almonds
Lamb and spinach
Lamb with yoghurt and coriander
Escalopes cooked on a hot stone
Lucknow leg of lamb
Lamb biryani
Parsi lamb with straw potatoes

Indian cheese
Cheese balls with potatoes and peas
Indian cheese, mushrooms and peas
Cheese in a spicy sauce
Parsi scrambled eggs

Lemon pullao with cashew nuts
Harvest rice
Rice with morels
Yoghurt rice
Mint Pullao
Yellow spring rice

Flat griddle bread
Bread stuffed with spiced potatoes
Potato cakes
Punjabi corn bread
Fried puffed bread
Wholewheat rolls

Coriander mint and yoghurt chutney
Walnut chutney
Sweet lemon pickle
Mint chutney
Cucumber raita
Spinach raita

Yoghurt and saffron cream
Perfumed ground rice
Mango mousse

# Acknowledgements

*I*n the fifteen years I spent teaching English at St. George's School, Rome, the Indian students, and their parents, freely indulged my passion for India, and I spent hours listening to their reminiscences and watching them cook. Mr. and Mrs. Muthoo, from Kashmir, and Mr. and Mrs. Joshi, from Delhi made helpful, encouraging suggestions when I first started travelling in India and Indira Joshi, Reshma Saigal, Rakesh Muthoo and Vivanyak Bhattacharjee, all former students, made India come alive for me even before my first visit. I am indebted to Dr. Antonio Capalbi, who shares my love of India, for his company during some of my travels and his support and patience during the writing of this book.

While researching this book in India, however, I met many distinguished Indian writers on food and chefs in leading restaurants throughout India, who were unfailingly helpful and invited me into their kitchens to see and understand fully how to achieve some of their special recipes. In Delhi, I would like to thank J. Inder Singh Kalra who generously led me through the labyrinth of Indian cooking. His book, 'Prashad – Cooking with the Indian Masters' proved invaluable during my Indian travels and I turn to it frequently when I am at home in Italy. He is a witty, erudite guide to India's great cultural and culinary heritage.

I am also indebted to Mrs. Bhicoo Manekshaw, a whirlwind of energy. She cooks, lectures and writes with endearing enthusiasm and gladly shares her expertise. Indira Gandhi asked her to teach her daughters-in-law to cook and I, too, was grateful for her clear instructions and down-to-earth approach. Her daughter, Mrs. Erna Chandra, was equally generous.

Also in Delhi, at the Taj Mahal Hotel, Vinati Mighra Berry, Ronnie Lobo and Harish Mathur were very helpful to me and Camilo D'Silva's 'Captain's Cabin' restaurant produced marvellous Goan specialities for me to sample. At the Taj Palace Hotel, Arvind Bhargava, the chef at the Handi restaurant and Arvind Sarawat, who is in charge of all the Taj restaurant hotels in north India welcomed me into their kitchens. At the Maurya Sheraton, Manjit Gill, the executive chef, showed me the delights of the Bokhara Grills and prepared Lucknow and Hyderabad specialities in the Dum Phukt restaurant while Charon Mann and his family extended their hospitality to me. My thanks also to Sunil Chandra, the general manager of the Oberoi, and to Jasjit Singh of the Imperial Hotel.

In Bombay, my thanks are due to Ms Mumtaz Currim, the well-known cookery writer, and Ms Meher Moos of the Government of India Tourist Office. Mrs S. N. Sonawala and Mrs A. G. Sonawala both extended to me their kind hospitality. Mrs. I. Knanna (T.C.I.) was helpful in her advice about the Andaman Islands.

At the Taj Hotel, my thanks go to Camellia Panjabi who kindly arranged for the cooperation of many of the Taj hotels and restaurants, while Umaima Mulla Feroze, editor of the Taj magazines, and the general manager, Subhir Bhowmick, were both very helpful. M. A. Kulkarni, manager of the Tanjore restaurant and Hemani Oberoi, the executive chef, invited me into their kitchens and Nisheeth Tak and Udit Sarkhel were also immensely helpful. At the Hotel President, Walter d'Rosario and Sampath Kumar, both chefs, receive my thanks.

In Madras, Cyrus Elavia, formerly executive chef at the Coromandel Hotel, and now a chef in Sydney, Australia, introduced me to the gastronomy of

Madras, showing me local markets, shops, kitchens and recipes. V. Suresh, the chef at the Mysore restaurants also receives my thanks. Jose Mascarenjas, the manager of the Fisherman's Cove Hotel at Covelong Beach, provided me with ideas and Ananda Reddy, chef at their restaurant, demonstrated new techniques and recipes with good humoured patience. Srijeeb Ray, of the Rain Tree restaurant at the Connemara Hotel, instructed me in Chettinad cooking in his very fine restaurant.

In Goa, my thanks must go to Thomas Braganza, chef of the Taj Holiday village, to Salil Dutt and to A. M. H. Mubarak Ali of the Hotel Mandoovi. In Jaipur, Mohammad Islam, formerly the cook to the Maharajah of Jaipur and now chef at the Rambagh Palace hotel, was extremely helpful. My thanks also go to V. Singh, the general manager of the Rambagh Palace hotel. K. K. Sood, the chef at the Jai Mahal Palace put his expertise at my disposal and gave generous advice. Mrs. Vatsala Singh and her husband explained the background of Rajasthan. In Jodhpur at the Agit Bhawan Hotel, Rani Usha Devi must receive my thanks for her kind hospitality and generous advice. Maharaj Swaroop Singh of the Ajir Bhawan hotel took me into the desert of Rajasthan to observe the local cooking and bread making. Sunder Singh and all his family shared their culinary expertise. In Mysore, my thanks go to R. Venkatesh chef at the Lalitha Mahal Palace, in Lucknow to Shashi Kapoor, in Cochin to S. Koder and A. M. Mukundan Nair, as well as K. Selvarajan, chef at the Malabar hotel. Lastly, I owe a deep debt of gratitude to Cyrus Todiwala, former executive chef at Fort Aguada Hotel in Goa, who spent days explaining Goan and Parsi dishes to me; he now runs The Place restaurant in Poona.

As well as those who helped me during my journeys and researches in India, Subhash Thaker, director of sales and marketing for the Taj International hotels, and his staff at the St. James' Court Hotel in London helped me with arranging many of my complicated appointments in India. Also in London, I would like to thank Mrs. Pushpa Prashar, who created Indian breads of smoothness and exquisite shape to inspire Robert Budwig in his drawings; also Shaheen Roohi Rashind.

As always, my thanks to Robert Budwig for the vibrant charm and colour of his drawings. In India I saw him bewitched by the visual feast spread before him and his drawings suggest the spell India weaves about us all.

Maureen Green, my editor, has been enthusiastic and supportive, Norma MacMillan has copy-edited with her usual thoroughness and Pamela Burden has typed and re-typed the manuscript.

Diane Seed, Rome 1990

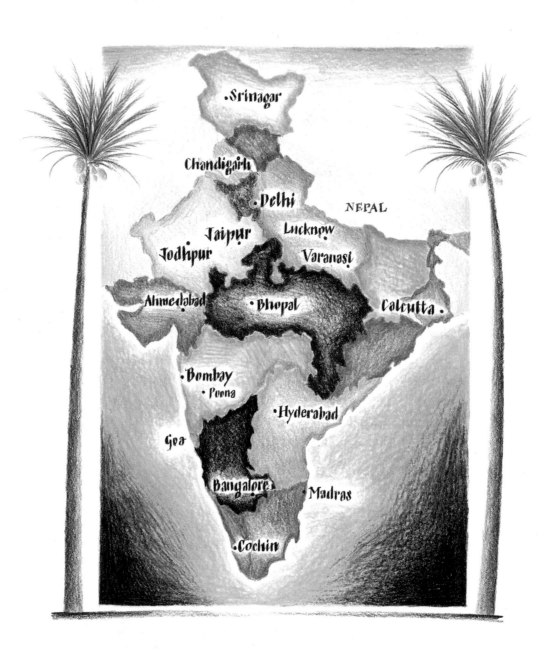

Srinagar

Chandigarh

Delhi

NEPAL

Jaipur          Lucknow

Jodhpur          Varanasi

Ahmedabad     ·Bhopal          Calcutta·

·Bombay
· Poona
                    ·Hyderabad

Goa

Bangalore          Madras

·Cochin

# Introduction

*I*ndian food can be simple or elaborate, frugal or opulent, but with a few basic ingredients, anyone can produce a good Indian dish that is worthy of Annapurna, the Hindu goddess of food.

My fascination with India first grew from literature and for many years I read every book about India that came to hand. I loved Indian food but I was for a while intimidated by the long list of alien spices and strange cooking utensils, and the wealth and variety of the culinary traditions of the many different states of the Indian sub-continent. The descriptions in many Indian cookery books of the time-honoured Indian extended family working together to produce the traditional wide selection of dishes also made me pause.

However, while I was researching this book, I came to realise that times have changed all over the world, even in India, and that many Indian housewives working outside the home, have had to make the same sort of practical compromises that women in Europe, in the United States and Australia have had to make. Nostalgic descriptions of British homes fragrant with the scent of freshly baked bread and cakes, or of Italian kitchens festooned with sheets of homemade golden pasta give as false an impression as Indian cookery books full of descriptions of family servants who spend each day grinding spices for elaborate dishes. In India today, in households without domestic help, good traditional food is still prepared, but the more complicated and exotic dishes are reserved for special occasions. And with the arrival of modern aids to cooking such as electric coffee grinders, which can pulverise spices within seconds, and food processors which turn chopping basic mixtures of garlic and ginger or making the dough for Indian bread into the work of a very few minutes, Indian food is within the reach of everyone.

## The influences on Indian food

The regional food of the vast sub-continent of India is the result of a complex contrast of races, religions and climate. The cooking of the cool Himalayas and Kashmir in the North of India, with its locally produced lamb and basmati rice from the northern plains, contrasts totally with the tropical diet of the fishing villages of Goa and the Malabar Coast on the Equator, where fish and shellfish cooked in blends of coconut are delicious specialities. As well as variations in climate, the north of India experienced centuries of conquest from warriors who made much less of an impact on the South. For this reason, and especially because of the conquest of the Moghuls, Muslim princes of Turkish and Persian origin, the food of northern India underwent a period of exquisite refinement. The cuisine brought to India by the great Moghul emperors and enjoyed at their courts, along with the art and architecture that they left to India, offered elegant creamy sauces of subtle flavour and combinations of saffron scented meat and rice.

Alongside the rich influences of climate and conquest, the religions of India have also determined the development of Indian food. Powerful taboos on what may or may not be eaten have been set down and practised for centuries by millions of Hindus, Muslims, Buddhists, Jainists and Sikhs and even the minority religions of Christianity, Judaism, and Zoroastrianism have contributed different and interesting cooking styles. Hindus and Sikhs do not eat beef, Muslims and Jews do not eat pork, Brahmins and Jains among Hindus are vegetarians of the strictest kind and do not eat fish or eggs either. Some will not eat red foods such as tomatoes, because of the resemblance of flesh. Others will not eat garlic or onions because they are strong flavours thought to inflame passions. Like all prohibitions, this has only served to increase the ingenuity of cooks.

## Indian spices and basic ingredients

The unique gift of Indian cooking to the world is its exploration and refinement of the flavourings and scents of spices. By roasting, grinding and frying an almost infinite combination of natural berries, pods, seeds and roots, the regions of India have developed a style of cooking that is recognised throughout the world.

Traditionally these spices were used to preserve food as well as give flavour. Many spices were prized for their medicinal qualities and are used, for example, in dishes of pulses to combat any tendency to flatulence. There are cold weather spices, like cinnamon, and hot weather flavours like tamarind that are used to give comfort. Mace, for example, is avoided in Indian cooking in the height of summer, since it is thought to provoke nose bleeds.

Indian cooking gains its endless variety from the subtle blending of spices, and their use varies from region to region. Travelling through India, I discovered five different prawn curries, each a different colour, texture and flavour because of the varying proportions of spices used. Because spices are the heart of Indian cooking, commercially prepared 'curry powders' should be strenuously avoided by anyone who wishes to approach real Indian food, since they make each dish taste boringly the same as any other. Instead, whole spices should be bought in small quantities (they begin to lose their strength after about three months) and dry roasted in a heavy pan before being ground to powder. A small electric coffee grinder is the ideal spice mill, even though purists talk of the superiority of a pestle and mortar. If planning to get thoroughly involved in Indian cooking, it is worth going to this little effort with the electric grinder. However, for the beginner, it is very possible to buy small tins of vacuum-packed ground spices which give quite pleasing results. In the same way, no one should be put off by the long list of spice ingredients in

some of the following recipes. Each spice adds an individual touch to a finished dish but it is a pity not to try a particular recipe because one more rare and optional flavouring such as asafetida is not to hand.

*Cinnamon*

Very little can be achieved without access to garlic, fresh root ginger and fresh green chillies, but items can be added to the spice cupboard gradually. Nutmeg, mace, cloves and cinnamon are all familiar to most cooks and after that cumin, coriander, turmeric, cardomom and cayenne pepper are the most essential. If you can find fresh coriander, the Indian equivalent of parsley in many recipes, their fragrant leaves are the authentic finishing touch to many dishes.

## The Spice Cupboard

**Asafoetida** (*Heeng*)
A resin, usually used in a pea-sized quantity, can be ground and used instead of onion in some recipes.

**Cardamom** (*Elaichi*)
Pods, black or green, which contain fragrant seeds, used extensively in meat, rice and desserts whole or ground. The seeds are extracted and ground, or more usually the whole pod is ground to produce a mild fragrance and flavour.

**Carom** (*Ajwain*)
Seeds with a sharp flavour added to vegetable dishes and breads, but to be used in moderation.

**Cinnamon** (*Dalchini*)
The bark of the cassia tree, or the smoother bark of the cin-namon

*Red pepper*

tree are both used as a flavouring whole or in powder form to add to many dishes, including Moghul rice.

**Clove** (*Laung*)
A dried bud, with powerful flavour and scent, used whole or ground in rice dishes and sauces.

**Coriander** (*Dhania*)
Both the seeds and the leaves of this essential plant are used. The strong scent and sweet flavour of the seeds used whole or ground, supply one of the most important of all spices in Indian cooking. Coriander is also a fresh herb used extensively as a garnish.

**Cumin** (*Jeera*)
Dried seeds, white or black, resembling caraway supply a nutty flavour and powerful scent. Used whole or ground in a wide range of Indian food, this is one of the most important of all Indian spices.

**Fennel** (*Saunf*)
The green seeds with sweet aniseed flavour and light scent, are used whole or ground in meat, rice and vegetable dishes.

**Fenugreek** (*Methi*)
The seeds provide a bitter flavour and powerful scent and are used whole or ground in vegetable and lentil dishes. Fenugreek is also used as a fresh herb.

### Ginger (*Adrak*)
Fresh root ginger, a powerfully scented rhizome, is used peeled and chopped finely in a wide variety of Indian recipes.

### Mace (*Javitri*)
The membrane surrounding the fruit of the nutmeg tree, stronger in flavour than nutmeg, and used in blade or ground powder form.

### Mustard seed (*Pai*)
The small black seeds of the mustard plant are used whole and ground as flavouring in most savoury dishes.

### Nutmeg (*Jaiphal*)
This dark brown fruit, a familiar scent in all cooking, with a sweet flavour, is used grated freshly in vegetable and rice dishes.

### Paprika (*Deghi Mirch*)
A mild-flavoured red chilli powder, sweet rather than hot and valued for its colouring in Indian cooking.

### Poppy seed (*Khas-Khas*)
A white seed, used ground as a thickening agent rather than flavouring, in sauces. The more familiar black poppy seed can also be used.

### Red pepper or cayenne (*Lal Mirch*)
A commercial blend of ground sun-dried chilli pods, hot in flavour and an adjunct of other flavourings. Take care in handling, as with all chillis, since it burns the skin.

### Saffron (*Kesar*)
Dried stigmas of a form of crocus plant, orange-red in colour are picked for their sweet scent and flavour. Saffron is best bought as threads because saffron powder frequently contains impurities. Expensive but alluring, a very small quantity flavours a meat or rice dish. Soak the threads in a little hot milk to free the colour and scent before adding to dish.

### Tamarind (*Imli*)
The pulpy pod, dark brown in colour, of the tamarind tree is preserved and sold commercially in a block like dates. The sour flavour is added to many

*Kari or curry leaves*

South India dishes. To use, soak a 50g / 2oz piece of tamarind paste in 250ml / 8fl oz boiling water, then mash it to extract the flavour. Strain the juice and use in cooking, or add the softened paste as directed.

### Turmeric (*Haldi*)
Like ginger, this is a short rhizome which is boiled and powdered and gives an intense yellow colour to vegetable, rice and meat dishes, as well as a strong woody flavour, and mild scent. Turmeric, bought ready ground, is the most important spice in Indian vegetarian food.

## Spice mixtures

*Garam masala:*

Tins of *garam masala* are commercially available but the homemade mixture gives a much more vivid flavour to this piquant spice mix.

  15ml / 1 tbsp green cardamom pods
  1 cinnamon stick 7.5cm / 3in long
  7.5ml / ½ tbsp whole cloves
  15g / ½oz black peppercorns
  30g / 1oz cumin seeds
  30g / 1oz coriander seeds

Dry roast the spices in a heavy frying pan without oil of any kind until they turn brown. Stir and shake throughout this process so that they do not burn. When cool, grind to a powder in an electric coffee grinder. Store in an airtight container.

*Sambhar masala:*

A spice blend used in South Indian cooking. Tins of this mixture, which contains turmeric, coriander, cayenne, fenugreek, cumin and pulses, are commercially available. The flavour is even better if made at home:

  60g / 2oz coriander seeds
  12 whole red dry chilli peppers
  8ml / 1½ tsp cumin seeds
  8ml / 1½ tsp black peppercorns
  8ml / 1½ tsp fenugreek seeds
  8ml / 1½ tsp white split gram beans
    (*urad dal*)
  8ml / 1½ tsp yellow mung beans
    (*moong dal*)
  8ml / 1½ tsp yellow split peas (*channa dal*)
  30ml / 2 tbsp turmeric

Put the first five ingredients to dry roast in a heavy frying pan without oil of any kind, stirring constantly so that they do not burn. After 5 minutes remove to a bowl and cool. Then dry roast all the beans and lentils for 5 to 10 minutes over a moderate heat. Remove to a bowl and cool. Add the turmeric to the warm pan and turn off the gas so that this spice simply warms. When all the ingredients are cool, grind in an electric grinder and store in an airtight container.

# Herbs & other basic ingredients

### Chick Pea Flour (*Besan*)

This flour made from chick peas (*garbanzos*) is also called gram flour and '*farine de pois chiches*' in many specialist shops. *Besan* is important in batters, sauces and breads.

### Corn or maize (*Makka*)

Corn or maize is grown throughout India, and the yellow flour is used for breads, cooked on the griddle.

### Green chilli pepper (*Hari Mirch*)

Fresh hot green chillipeppers come in varying strengths, the smaller the pod, the hotter. Slice open and scrape out the seeds before chopping but handle with care as they are dangerous to skin and blinding to the eyes. Chillis keep well wrapped in the refrigerator for 2 to 3 weeks.

### Coconut (*Narial*)

The well-known fruit of the coconut palm. When buying judge freshness by weight: the liquid inside a fresh coconut makes it heavy. Apart from opening the coconut by brute force, it can be tackled by piercing the 'eyes' with a skewer, draining off the liquid, and heating in a moderate oven for 25 minutes; then tap to loosen the nut from the shell and open with a hard blow from a hammer. Release the meat from the shell with a knife.

*Grating a coconut:* cut the brown skin from the meat and grate in small pieces on a hand grater or in a food processor. Add the grated coconut to sauces and other dishes as directed.

*Coconut milk:* to make fresh coconut milk, add 250ml / 8fl oz hot water to

3oz / 90g / ¾ cup of grated coconut. Soak for an hour or more, then blend or process and strain off the liquid.

Cream of coconut (unsweetened) is readily available in block form in specialist shops and can be made into milk. Add ¼ pint /150ml / ⅔ cup of hot water to 75ml / 5 tbsp of creamed coconut and mash or blend into milk. Tinned coconut milk is also on sale.

### Coriander leaves (*Hara Dhania*)
Fresh, green coriander leaves, also called cilantro, are the parsley of Indian cooking, sprinkled as a garnish on many dishes, but sometimes used in quantity to provide a sharp green sauce. Rooted bunches can be kept in water in the refrigerator for several weeks.

### Dried Split Lentils/Peas, Beans (*Dal*)
Many different kinds of *dal* exist in Indian cooking, all easy to store and use but the names are sometimes varied in confusing ways. The most frequently used are:

yellow lentils (*toovar dal*)
pink lentils (*masar dal*)
mung beans (*moong dal*)
black gram beans (*urad dal*)
yellow split peas (*channa dal*)

But mung beans in their skins are referred to as green gram beans; only when hulled do they become the familiar yellow *moong dal*. Black gram beans are known as *sabat urad* when whole and dark, but as *urad dal* when hulled and white. Reassuringly, in many recipes one *dal* can be substituted for another with comparative ease.

### Indian clarified butter (*Ghee*)
This is obtainable from specialist stores in tins or can be made at home by heating fresh butter and simmering until the moisture evaporates from the solids. Then strain through muslin or cheesecloth into covered jars.

### Kari or curry leaves (*Meethe Neam Ke Patte*)
These bright green leaves, with bitter flavour and strong scent are difficult to obtain fresh, but they are usually available dried. The addition of *kari* leaves is typical of southern Indian cooking.

# Menu building

Working out how to fit together an Indian meal is sometimes a problem for those beginning to cook Indian food. But whether the meal is vegetarian or non-vegetarian the same basic rules apply. Each Indian meal should consist of one main dish, for example, a meat, poultry or fish dish, or a lentil and vegetable combination; and this should be allied to a staple,

either rice or bread or both. If the meal is vegetarian, a yoghurt dish is usually added. And two side dishes of spicy vegetables one 'wet' and one 'dry' as well as some pickle or chutney will also be on offer. The more elaborate the party, the more alternatives to these dishes will be prepared. For a simple supper perhaps only two, such as a soup and bread, or a lentil and vegetable recipe and rice, are needed. So what can seem a style of cooking bewildering in its variety, can come down to something as simple as a combination of bread stuffed with spiced potatoes and a bowl of mulligatawny soup. And very delicious that can be.

However, I must say, as I travelled around India, studying recipes and cooking techniques, I was continually having newly learned information on this topic turned upside down and often flatly contradicted. This is inevitable in a country as vast as India and made up of so many different cultures and religions. And one of the current battles being fought on the culinary front in fashionable restaurants and in elegant homes in Delhi is that of the 'thali' versus separate 'courses'. I had learned that 'courses' as such do not really exist in traditional Indian cooking and I had adapted very happily to the 'thali' or flat metal tray where all the dishes on offer are served in small portions in little metal bowls together with small quantities of bread and rice. But in Delhi, Mr. J. Inder Singh Kalra, the doyen of elegant Indian food and a noted writer on the subject, firmly believes that an Indian meal should be served course by course, beginning with traditional kebabs. This culinary philosophy is followed in the Wellcome Group's new 'Dum Phukt' restaurant in Delhi. So it seems perfectly acceptable to serve an Indian meal course by course or all at the same time, whichever you prefer. Traditionally, bread was served as the staple in northern India and rice in the South. Today, the boundaries have become blurred and both are often served together.

I find a complete Indian meal a good way of entertaining a large group of friends, but for my family cooking I often make an Indian soup and bread by themselves, or even a one-dish vegetable and lentil combination. Indian cooking can be very flexible and fit in with the needs of every occasion.

Indian food may only rarely be classified as fast food, although a simple dish of Parsi scrambled eggs is a feast within minutes. In India I learned some labour-saving tricks that have made my life considerably easier. Before starting to prepare an Indian feast I now process quantities of peeled garlic and ginger separately in my processor to make a thick paste which will keep well in the fridge for forty eight hours. This paste will even freeze quite well. This saves repeating the rather tedious procedure and it is much easier to prepare in bulk. But the great boon of Indian cooking for the busy modern hostess or family cook is that Indian food tastes even better the day after: the flavour of the spices seems to deepen and become more complex after resting for twenty four hours, so that meat and even fish recipes are very suitable for preparing the day before and re-heating shortly before guests arrive. Also, when I have small quantities of a tasty main dish left over, I freeze it and use it at a later date to make an original stuffing for samosas.

**Please Note**
*All recipes in
this book serve 6.*

# Appetizers, Soups & Snacks

*I*ndians love to eat and every region of India is rich in snacks that can be enjoyed at any hour of the day or night. These make interesting cocktail nibbles, or a small selection can be served as an original first course. The British first introduced the concept of 'soup' to Indian cooking and over the years many delicious soups have become an inherent part of an Indian meal. However, many Indians believe that appetizers are an alien innovation, so the options for the international cook are explained more fully in the section on meal planning.

# Mulligatawny Soup
## *Mulligatanni*

This very popular, elegant soup was invented in Madras about two hundred years ago. The name, in Tamil, means 'pepper water'. There are many vegetarian and non-vegetarian versions, but my favourite recipe comes from the restaurant of the Fisherman's Cove Hotel at Covelong on the Coromandel coast. This hotel is built on a long white beach near a small fishing village near Mahabalipuram, with its spectacular monolithic monuments and romantic eighth century Shore Temple.

**200g / 7oz (1 cup) split orange lentils (*masoor dal*)**
**1 litre / 1¾ pints (1 quart) light stock (e.g. chicken)**
**100g / 3½oz potato**
**100g / 3½oz apple**
**20ml / 1½ tbsp vegetable oil**
**100g / 3½oz onion**
**5 cloves garlic**
**4cm / 1½ inch square fresh root ginger**
**1 fresh hot green chilli pepper**
**3cm / 1½ inch stick cinnamon**
**5 cloves**
**10ml / 2 tsp ground coriander**
**5ml / 1 tsp ground cumin**
**5ml / 1 tsp turmeric**
**5 fresh or dried curry leaves**
**50g / 2oz creamed coconut mixed with 250 ml / 8 fl oz boiling water**
**40ml / 2½ tbsp fresh lemon juice**
**5ml / 1 tsp salt**
**30ml / 2 tbsp chopped coriander leaves**

Wash and pick over the lentils then put them in a saucepan with the stock and bring to the boil. Slice the potato and apple add to the lentils, and cook for about 20 minutes or until all are soft. Heat the oil and gently fry the finely-chopped onion, garlic, ginger and seeded green chilli pepper. When the onion is soft, add the spices and curry leaves. Cook, stirring continuously, until the oil comes out of the spice mixture. Remove the whole spices and purée the mixture. Purée the lentil, apple and potato mixture, and stir in the coconut 'milk' and the puréed spice mixture. Add the lemon juice and salt, and taste for seasoning. Before serving, garnish with the chopped coriander leaves.

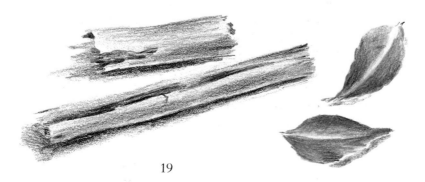

# Chilled Avocado & Coconut Soup
### *Moplas Soup*

The Malabar coast with its exotic spices and lush green vegetation has attracted intrepid foreign traders since the beginning of time. Hundreds of years ago some Arab merchants succumbed to the local siren song, intermarried and became known as the *moplas* or sons-in-law. It is to them we owe this deliciously cool soup

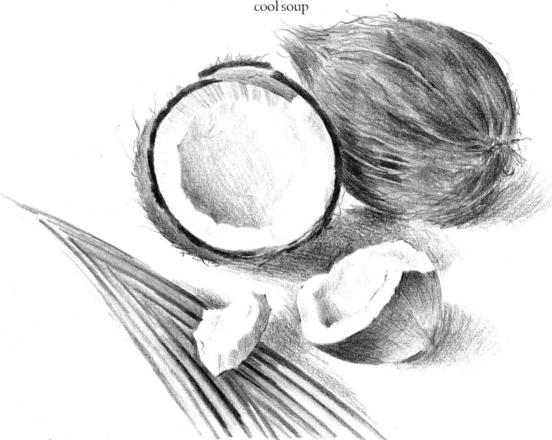

1 large ripe avocado
100g / 3½oz (1 cup) freshly grated coconut
250ml / 8fl oz plain yoghurt
30ml / 2 tbsp lemon juice
3 small cloves garlic
4 fresh hot green chilli peppers
5ml / 1 tsp ground cumin
750ml / 1¼ pints (3 cups) water
salt
30ml / 2 tbsp chopped fresh coriander leaves

Put the peeled, stoned avocado into a food processor, together with the grated coconut, yoghurt, lemon juice, garlic, seeded chilli peppers and cumin. Add a little of the water and work to make a smooth paste. Blend in the rest of the water, and add salt to taste.
Serve chilled, with freshly-chopped coriander leaves sprinkled on top.

# Shellfish Soup
## *Sopa Grossa*

Goa, with its many different races and religions living happily together, has an exciting, varied cuisine. The Portuguese ruled here for 450 years and part of their influence can be seen in the Latin names of many dishes. All Goans love seafood, and this recipe uses local shellfish to enrich the villagers' sustaining rice gruel called *pez*. Every household has its own variation of the soup, and you can use whatever shellfish is to hand: I have successfully used a mixture of mussels, prawns or shrimps and squid. If any fish still in its shell is available, it will give the soup a richer flavour.

1kg / 2¼lb mixed shellfish, with or without shells, fresh or frozen
200ml / 7fl oz white wine
500ml / 16fl oz water
45ml / 3 tbsp vegetable oil
1 large onion, finely chopped
15ml / 1 tbsp finely chopped garlic
15ml / 1 tbsp finely chopped fresh root ginger
2.5ml / ½ tsp turmeric
5ml / 1 tsp cumin seeds
5ml / 1 tsp coriander seeds
175g / 6oz (1 cup) cooked rice

Cook the fresh shellfish in the wine and water until the shells open or the fish is just cooked; if using frozen shellfish, thaw and then simmer in the wine and water until cooked. Discard the shells of fresh shellfish, if any, and filter the liquid through muslin or cheesecloth to remove any sand. In a food processor chop the shellfish but do not reduce to a purée. Heat the oil and fry the finely chopped onion until soft. Add the garlic, ginger and spices, and fry for a few minutes on a low heat stirring constantly. Add the chopped shellfish, cooked rice and cooking liquid, with salt to taste and heat through gently.

# Spinach & Cream Soup
*Palak Shorba*

In India, spinach appears in many guises. Here spinach and rice are combined with chicken stock to make a delicate, fragrant green soup.

1kg / 2¼lb fresh spinach or equivalent quantity frozen spinach
30ml / 2 tbsp vegetable oil
1 clove garlic
300g / 10oz onions
5ml / 1 tsp each ground mace, cumin and black pepper
1.25ml / ¼ tsp ground cloves
2.5ml / ½ tsp ground cinnamon
60g / 2½oz (½ cup) cooked rice (page 97)
750ml / 1¼ pints (3 cups) chicken stock
salt and black pepper
200ml / 7fl oz milk
45ml / 3 tbsp cream
20ml / 1½ tbsp lemon juice

Heat the oil and fry the finely sliced onions and finely chopped garlic until they are slightly coloured. Add the ground spices and stir for a few minutes, then remove from the heat.

Cook the spinach until wilted, then drain well. Purée the cooked rice and spinach in a food processor or blender with a little of the stock, then add the sliced onions and purée again. Pour this mixture into a pan together with the rest of the stock. Add salt to taste, the milk and cream. Heat the soup, stirring occasionally taking care not to let it boil. Just before serving, add the lemon juice and black pepper to taste.

# Spiced Yoghurt Soup
## *Dahi Ka Shorba*

I first sampled this soup at the Taj Palace Hotel in Delhi, and it became one of my favourites. Quick and easy, the first stage can be prepared in advanced.

750ml / 1¼ pints (3 cups) plain yoghurt
100ml / 3½fl oz cream
50g / scant 2oz (3½ tbsp) butter
30g / 1oz onion
30g / 1oz peeled tomatoes
1 fresh hot green chilli pepper
15ml / 1 tbsp finely chopped fresh root ginger
15ml / 1 tbsp cumin seeds
5ml / 1 tsp turmeric powder
30g fresh coriander leaves
salt

Chop the onions, ginger, tomatoes and seeded chilli peppers. Heat the butter, add the cumin seeds and let them start to crackle before adding the chopped vegetables and turmeric. Cook for about 15 minutes. Remove from the heat and allow to cool, then purée in a blender. Just before serving, add the yoghurt, cream, coriander leaves and salt to taste and heat gently. Do not allow to boil.

# Tomato & Coconut Cream Soup
## *Tamatar Ka Shorba*

This quick, easy soup from Bombay can be used to tempt conservative palates since it is the old favourite, cream of tomato soup, with a subtle difference.

400g / 14oz tin plum tomatoes
30g / 1¼oz creamed coconut dissolved in 250ml / 8fl oz hot water
5ml / 1 tsp sugar
5ml / 1 tsp salt
30ml / 2 tbsp vegetable oil
5ml / 1 tsp ground coriander
5ml / 1 tsp ground cumin
2.5ml / ½ tsp cayenne pepper
1 fresh hot green chilli pepper
15ml / 1 tbsp rice flour
black pepper
3 tbsp / ⅓oz (¼ cup) fresh coriander leaves

Cook the tomatoes with the sugar and salt, crushing occasionally with a spoon, until they are slightly reduced. Purée adding the rice flour. Heat the oil and add the ground coriander, cumin, cayenne pepper and seeded and finely chopped green chilli pepper, and cook for a few minutes. Stir in the coconut 'milk' and puréed tomatoes. Simmer, stirring, until slightly thickened. Season to taste with black pepper. Before serving, garnish with the chopped coriander leaves.

# Pumpkin & Courgettes Kofta
## *Ghia Kofta*

This recipe comes from the holy Hindu city of Benares, famous for its variety of vegetarian delicacies. Garlic is omitted although a small quantity of onion is used: traditionally, high Brahmins among Hindus avoid not only meat but also strong flavours like garlic and onion which are thought to inflame the passions. The kofta can be made with one vegetable only, but I like the colourful orange and green streaks obtained by mixing pumpkin and courgette.

500g / 1lb 2oz pumpkin
500g / 1lb 2oz courgettes (zucchini)
100)g / 3½oz onion
2 fresh hot green chilli peppers
1cm / ½ inch piece fresh root ginger
100g / 3½oz (1 cup) chick pea flour (*besan*)

20g / ⅔oz (½ cup) chopped coriander
  leaves
15ml / 1 tbsp ground cumin
15ml / 1 tbsp ground coriander
5ml / 1 tsp salt
vegetable oil for deep frying

The pumpkin and courgettes (zucchini) can be put through the julienne disc of a food processor or grated together with the onion. Remove the seeds from the chilli peppers and the peel from the ginger and chop both very finely. Mix in all the other ingredients. Mould the mixture into small balls and place them on a slightly tilted chopping board so that the excess moisture runs out. Leave to drain for an hour. Just before frying, squeeze out any remaining excess moisture and gently re-form the balls. Heat the oil in a deep pan to 190°C / 375°F. Fry the kofta a few at a time. Remove with a slotted spoon and drain on kitchen paper. Serve immediately, or re-fry in hot oil for a few minutes just before serving.

# Samosas
## *Samosas*

These are probably the best known Indian snacks; however, the often soggy pastries found in shops outside India bear no resemblance to crisp, freshly-made samosas. Traditionally, they are either stuffed with minced (ground) lamb or peas and potatoes, but I often freeze left-over small portions of other Indian dishes and afterwards prepare a dry paste to fill samosas when a different main dish is being served. In the same way, I am often happier with my familiar shortcrust pastry, which for me simplifies making samosas, rather than using this Indian pastry.

**Pastry (Indian)**
300g / 10oz (2 cups) plain (all purpose) flour
60ml / 4 tbsp vegetable oil
pinch of salt

**Potato Filling**
750g / 1¾lb potatoes
250g / 9oz (1⅔ cups) shelled peas
30ml / 2 tbsp vegetable oil
10ml / 2 tsp cumin seeds
1 medium onion
4cm / 1½ inch piece fresh root ginger
4 fresh hot green chilli peppers
5ml / 1 tsp salt
5ml / 1 tsp cayenne pepper
30g / 1¼oz (⅔ cups) fresh coriander leaves

Sift the flour and salt into a bowl. Rub in the oil until the mixture is like fine breadcrumbs, then slowly add about 90ml / 6 tbsp water to make a stiff dough.
Put the dough in an oiled plastic bag and let it rest for at least 30 minutes. Meanwhile, make the filling. Heat the oil and let the cumin seeds spatter for a few minutes before adding the finely chopped onion and ginger. Cook until they begin to soften. Add the potatoes cut into small cubes and the seeded chilli peppers cut into fine rings. Stir in the salt and about 100ml / 3½fl oz water. Cover and simmer until the potatoes are cooked. If you are using frozen peas, add them to the mixture and cook for a further 4 minutes. Fresh peas need no further cooking. Stir in the cayenne pepper and chopped coriander. Allow to cool. Roll out the dough and cut into about 18 large circles. Cut each circle in half and fold over to form a cone. Seal the long edge with water and, using a fork, press down on the seam to make it stronger. Lift up the cone, open it out and fill it with the potato mixture or another filling. Do not fill it too full or it will be difficult to repeat the sealing procedure with the top.
Deep fry the samosas until they are golden brown. Drain on kitchen paper and serve immediately.

# Fish Croquettes
*Kofta Shami Machi*

I don't know the origin of these fish croquettes, but they make a delectable cocktail snack or appetizer. I often serve them with mint chutney before a European meal.

400g / 14oz skinned white fish fillet
50g / 2oz (¼ cup) yellow split peas *(channa dal)*
4 whole green cardamom pods
2cm / ¾ inch stick cinnamon
15ml / 1 tbsp white poppy seeds
salt
15ml / 1 tbsp black pepper
1 egg white
150ml / 5fl oz plain yoghurt
vegetable oil for deep frying

*Filling*
25g / 1oz (2 tbsp) butter
2 cloves garlic
10ml / 2 tsp finely chopped fresh root ginger
150g / 5oz shelled raw prawns (shrimp)
2.5ml / ½ tsp carom *(ajwain)*
5ml / 1 tsp black pepper
salt

Soak the *channa dal* in water to cover for about an hour. Grind the spices and work together in a food processor with the fish, the drained *channa dal*, salt to taste and pepper to make a smooth paste. Add the egg white and yoghurt. Chill this paste for half an hour.

Heat the butter and gently cook the finely chopped garlic and ginger with the prawns (shrimp). Sprinkle in the carom, pepper and salt to taste. Work in the food processor to chop coarsely, but be careful not to over-process and form a paste.

Take the fish mixture from the refrigerator and divide into small balls. Flatten them in your hand and wrap around small balls of filling. When the filling is completely enclosed, roll into balls again. Fry in hot deep oil until crisp and golden, drain on kitchen paper and serve hot.

# Garnished Pappadams
## *Masala Papad*

I first fell in love with these at the Tanjore restaurant at the Taj Hotel, Bombay. Now ordinary pappadams seem quite insipid.

6 pappadams
oil for deep frying
freshly grated coconut
chopped coriander leaves
chilli powder

Heat the oil in a deep pan to 180°C / 350°F. Fry the pappadams one at a time for a few seconds. Drain on kitchen paper and sprinkle with coconut, coriander and chilli powder. Serve at once.

# Chicken & Cashew Nut Kebabs
## *Reshmi Kebab*

Ideal barbecue foods, these tasty kebabs come from the North West Frontier. They are served to perfection in the Maurya Sheraton's Bokhara restaurant in Delhi. They are spicy without being 'hot', and the cashew nuts provide a very interesting texture.

**1kg / 2¼lb fresh skinless boneless chicken**
**50g / 2oz shelled cashew nuts**
**2 eggs**
**20ml / 4 tsp vegetable oil**
**7.5ml / 1½ tsp cayenne pepper**
**7.5ml / 1½ tsp white pepper**
**30ml / 2 tbsp ground cumin**
**salt**
**20g / scant 1oz (1½ tbsp) onion**
**30g / 1¼oz fresh root ginger**
**20g / ⅔oz (½ cup) fresh coriander leaves**
**7.5ml / 1½ tsp *garam masala***

Mince (grind) the chicken and add the beaten eggs, oil, spices and salt to taste. Grind the nuts and finely chop the onion, peeled ginger and coriander leaves. Add to the chicken together with the *garam masala* and mix well to form a thick paste. Divide the mixture into six balls. Thread each on to a skewer and, with wet hands, spread the ball along the skewer to form a long, sausage-shape. Cook on a charcoal grill or in a preheated oven at 150°C / 300°F / gas 2 for 8 to 10 minutes, basting with a little extra oil to keep the kebabs moist.

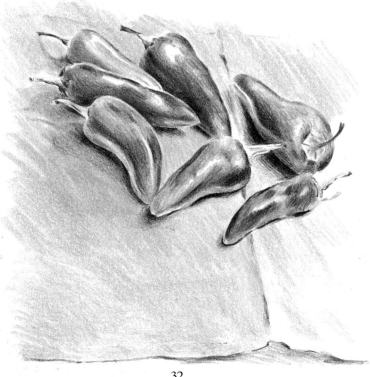

# Vegetable Fritters
### *Pakora*

This tasty snack is found all over India and seems to be eaten at any hour of the day or night. The fritters can be prepared well in advance, and then briefly re-fried just before serving. The first version here, in which each vegetable is coated separately, is a useful accompaniment to a main course. I like to serve the second version, which produces crisp balls of mixed vegetables, as tasty nibbles with cocktails before a dinner party.

**First version**
**Batter**
250g / 9oz (2¼ cups) chick pea flour (*besan*)
2.5ml / ½ tsp bicarbonate of soda (baking soda)
200ml / 7fl oz water
5ml / 1 tsp dried carom (*ajwain*) (optional)
5ml / 1 tsp cayenne pepper
5ml / 1 tsp salt
vegetable oil for deep frying

**Vegetables**
150g / 5oz cauliflower
150g / 5oz onions
150g / 5oz courgettes (zucchini)
150g / 5oz potatoes
150g / 5oz aubergine (eggplant)

Mix all the batter ingredients together in a food processor. Divide the cauliflower into florets, and slice the other vegetables into rounds about 5mm / ¼ inch thick. Put the potatoes and aubergine (eggplant) in cold water until ready to fry (drain and pat dry before coating with batter).

Heat the oil in a deep pan to 190°C / 375°F. Dip the vegetables into the batter and fry a few at a time until they are a pale gold colour. Remove with a slotted spoon and put to drain on kitchen paper.

Immediately before serving, reheat the oil to 150°C / 350°F and fry for a further 5 minutes or so, until the fritters are a crisp, deep brown. Drain again on kitchen paper, and serve.

### Second version
**Batter**
100g / 3½oz (scant 1 cup) chick pea flour (*besan*)
2.5ml / ½ tsp bicarbonate of soda (baking soda)
10ml / 2 tsp ground cumin
10ml / 2 tsp salt
5ml / 1 tsp cayenne pepper
150ml / 5fl oz water
vegetable oil for deep frying

**Vegetables**
100g / 3½oz potatoes
100g / 3½oz courgettes (zucchini)
50g / 2oz onion
20g / ⅔oz (½ cup) fresh coriander leaves

Mix together all the batter ingredients in a food processor. Stir in the grated potato and courgettes (zucchini), finely chopped onion and chopped coriander.

Heat the oil in a deep pan to 190°C / 375°F. Drop in large spoonfuls of the mixture. These will soon puff out and float on the oil. Use a slotted spoon to turn them over so that they become an even golden brown.

Drain on kitchen paper and either serve at once or, if prepared ahead, re-fry at 150°C / 350°F for a few minutes before serving.

# Kashmiri Meat Balls
## *Goolar Kebab*

These small, tasty meat balls are named after the Indian wild fig, the goolar.

500g / 1lb 2oz lean minced (ground) lamb
75g / 3oz (⅓ cup) yellow split peas (*channa dal*)
30g / 1¼oz (3 tbsp) onion
15ml / 1 tbsp finely chopped fresh root ginger
6 whole green cardamom pods
6 cloves
4cm / 1½ inch stick cinnamon
2 bay leaves
3 eggs
salt
30ml / 2 tbsp white poppy seeds
vegetable oil for deep frying

*Filling*
30g / 1¼oz (⅔ cup) fresh mint leaves
30g / 1¼oz (⅔ cup) fresh coriander leaves
4 fresh hot green chilli peppers
50g / 2oz (⅓ cup) raisins
30ml / 2 tbsp mixed grated orange and lemon rind
salt

Wash the *channa dal* and put it in a saucepan with the lamb, chopped onion, ginger, spices and bay leaves. Add 500ml / 16fl oz of water and bring to the boil. Simmer gently until the dal are cooked, then turn up the heat and let the remaining water evaporate so that the mixture is completely dry. Remove the spices and bay leaves and work in a food processor to a smooth paste. Beat 2 of the eggs into the mixture and add salt to taste. Put the paste into the refrigerator to become firm while you are preparing the filling.

Chop the mint and coriander and work to a coarse paste in a food processor with the seeded chilli peppers, raisins and rind. Salt to taste. Divide the filling into 20 portions, and do the same with the lamb mixture. Roll the lamb mixture into balls, then flatten one in your palm, using your thumb to make a dent in the middle. Push a ball of the filling into the dent, then mould the meat around it and shape into a ball again. If the mixture gets too sticky, wet your hands when moulding the balls.

Beat the remaining egg. Roll each completed ball in egg and then in poppy seeds to coat all over. Chill for at least half an hour, then deep fry in batches in hot oil until golden brown on all sides. Drain on kitchen paper and serve hot or cold.

# Tandoori Prawns
## *Tandoori Jhinga*

Served on sticks, these prawns make excellent pre-dinner nibbles.

18 large raw prawns (shrimp) in shell
salt
120ml / 4fl oz lemon juice
20g / scant 1oz (2 tbsp) butter (for basting)

**Marinade**
4 cloves fresh garlic
30g / 1¼oz fresh root ginger

250ml / 8fl oz plain yoghurt
2 eggs
50g / 2oz (½ cup) chick pea flour
 (*besan*)
20ml / 4 tsp cayenne pepper
15ml / 1 tbsp *garam masala*
pinch of asafoetida (optional)
few drops of orange food colouring
 (optional)

Remove the heads of the prawns (shrimp) and the vein along the back, but keep the tail shells intact. Pat dry, rub with salt and put in a bowl with half the lemon juice.

Put the peeled garlic and ginger into a food processor and work to make a thick paste, adding a little water. Add all the other marinade ingredients and blend briefly. Put the prawns to marinate in this mixture for several hours.

When ready to cook, drain the prawns, shaking off any excess marinating paste. Thread them onto six skewers, leaving a gap between each prawn. Grill (or broil) them on both sides, brushing them with melted butter to keep them moist. If preferred, the prawns can be cooked in a heavy frying pan or on a griddle. Sprinkle the remaining lemon juice over the prawns before serving.

# Vegetables & Pulses

*T*he richly varied traditions of vegetarian cooking in India have provided a prime attraction for many western cooks. Because a large proportion of the population, particularly in South India, are strict vegetarians, following the Hindu concept that a pure diet facilitates a pure mind, vegetables and pulses play a very important role in Indian cooking. The even stricter Jains avoid any root vegetable in case insects are killed when the vegetables are pulled from the earth, and some purists avoid blood-coloured vegetables like tomatoes and beetroot. Orthodox Brahmins even eschew onions and garlic because they are thought to inflame the passions in the same way as meat. These restrictions have encouraged local ingenuity in the kitchen.

As well as many vegetables available to western cooks, I discovered many unfamiliar vegetables in the Madras market, like drumstick and yard beans, and a bitter gourd which is served to diabetics to lower the sugar in the blood. An infinite variety of pulses are used throughout India to supply essential protein and green leafy vegetables are served at most meals. The recipes where lentils and vegetables are cooked together make deliciously subtle, healthy vegetarian fare.

# Aubergines with Apples & Pear
### *Tsoont Baingan*

Hindu Kasmiris usually cook this in the autumn using quinces or hard cooking pears. I like the flavour and texture produced by combining crisp, sour apples with a more mellow pear.

**6 medium-sized aubergines (eggplants)**
**2 tart apples**
**1 large pear**
**salt**
**5ml / 1 tsp fennel seeds**
**5ml / 1 tsp turmeric**
**10ml / 2 tsp cayenne pepper**
**100ml / 3½fl oz vegetable oil**
**pinch of asafoetida (optional)**

Cut the aubergines (eggplants) into slices about 3cm / 1¼ inch thick, sprinkle with salt and leave for at least an hour to 'purge'.
Grind the fennel seeds to powder and mix with the turmeric and cayenne pepper and a little water to make a paste. Rinse and dry the aubergine (eggplants) slices. Without removing the peel, cut the apples and pear into 8 segments each. Heat the oil, sprinkle on the asafoetida, then quickly brown the apple and pear segments.
Remove with a slotted spoon and put to drain on kitchen paper. Brown the aubergines (eggplants) slices in batches and put them to drain with the fruit. When all the slices have been browned pour off any remaining oil and return the apples, pears and aubergines (eggplants) to the pan. Gently stir in the spice paste cover and cook gently for 10 to 15 minutes. Check salt to taste.

# Aubergines with Tomato & Yoghurt
## *Badal Jaam*

This dish is always popular. One of my Italian friends claims that it seems a spicier version of *melanzane alla parmigiana*, the classic Italian aubergine dish.

800g / 1¾lb aubergines (eggplant)
400g / 14oz tin tomatoes
600ml / 1 pint (2½ cups) plain yoghurt
salt
vegetable oil
100g / 3½oz (1 cup) onion

8 cloves garlic
20g / ⅔oz fresh root ginger
5ml / 1 tsp cayenne pepper
30ml / 2 tbsp lemon juice
20g / ⅔oz (½ cup) fresh coriander
  leaves

Put the yoghurt to drain through muslin, or a fine sieve for at least 4 hours.
Slice the aubergines (eggplant) into 2cm / ¾ inch thick rounds, sprinkle with salt and leave to 'purge'.
Meanwhile, heat 25ml / 1½ tbsp oil and gently fry the sliced onion. Peel and chop the garlic and ginger, reserving 3 garlic cloves to be used in the yoghurt topping.
Add the chopped garlic, ginger and tomatoes to the onion and cook until the tomatoes are slightly reduced. Stir in the cayenne pepper and salt to taste.
Pat the aubergine (eggplant) slices dry, then fry in oil until browned on both sides.
Drain on kitchen paper and then arrange in one layer in a large, ovenproof dish.
Purée the tomato sauce in a blender or food processor and spoon over the aubergine (eggplant) slices. Cover the dish with tightly sealed foil. Place in a 180°C / 350°F / gas 4 oven to cook for 10 to 15 minutes.
Stir the remaining chopped garlic, lemon juice and chopped coriander into the drained yoghurt. Spoon over the aubergine (eggplant) just before serving.

# Swiss Chard with Mung beans

*Kootoo*

This is a Brahmin dish from the South. I find it works well with the thick stalks of Swiss chard.

1kg / 2¼lb Swiss chard
200g / 7oz (1 cup) mung beans (*moong dal*)
2.5ml / ½ tsp turmeric
200g / 7oz potatoes
10ml / 2 tsp *sambhar masala* (see page 14)
pinch of asafoetida (optional)
salt
4 fresh hot green chilli peppers
150g / 5oz (1½ cups) freshly grated coconut
10ml / 2 tsp cumin seeds
60ml / 4 tbsp vegetable oil
5ml / 1 tsp black mustard seeds
10 fresh or dried curry leaves

Wash the dal in running water, then put them to soak in water to cover for an hour. Drain and put with the turmeric and 500ml / 16fl oz water in a saucepan. Bring to the boil. Add the peeled, cubed potatoes and cook for about 20 minutes, with the lid half on.

Add the stalks of the chard, cut into pieces about 4cm / 1½ inches long, together with the *sambhar* spices, the asafoetida and a little salt. Cook for about 5 minutes, then add the chard leaves, cut into wide ribbons, and 500ml / 16fl oz of boiling water.

Purée the seeded chilli peppers, coconut and cumin seeds with a little water to make a thick paste and stir into the pan. Simmer for a few minutes longer. Heat the oil in a separate pan and scatter in the mustard seeds and curry leaves. Cook until the mustard seeds pop. Stir into the chard mixture and sprinkle with the chopped fresh coriander.

# Mixed Vegetables in Coconut Milk
## *Avial*

This has become one of my favourites and can be made with almost any
combination of vegetables. Traditionally served with 'Ven Pongal' rice, it is
equally good with any other rice. In the interests of healthy eating, I have slightly
changed the cooking process to avoid any initial frying.
I first ate this dish sitting on the lawn outside the Malabar Hotel in Cochin,
watching the rice barges glide past larger boats laden with cargoes
of exotic spices.

1 slice pumpkin, about 200g / 7oz
1 potato
3 carrots
3 large sweet peppers
1 large aubergine (eggplant)
6 courgettes (zucchini)
10 large green beans
salt
50g / 2oz (½ cup) grated fresh coconut
3 cloves garlic
2 fresh hot green chilli peppers
50g / 2oz creamed coconut mixed with 250ml / 8fl oz boiling water
6 fresh or dried curry leaves

Peel the vegetables if necessary and cut into sticks about 5cm / 2 inches long. Boil
in a pan of salted water, one at a time, until the vegetables are barely cooked. It is
important that they retain their firm texture. Keep the cooking liquid.
Blend the coconut, garlic and seeded chilli peppers with a little water in a food
processor. Add to the vegetable stock, then stir in the thick coconut 'milk'. Bring
almost to the boil, then add the cooked vegetables and curry leaves. Check for
seasoning. Simmer very gently for about 5 minutes before serving.

# Spiced Potatoes
## *Aloo Dum*

500g / 1lb 2oz small potatoes
30ml / 2 tbsp vegetable oil
3 cloves
1 bay leaf
2 whole green cardamom pods
5ml / 1 tsp turmeric
5ml / 1 tsp salt
1 medium onion
3 cloves garlic
2cm / ¾ inch piece fresh root ginger

2 fresh hot green chilli peppers
15ml / 1 tbsp lemon juice
3cm / 1¼ inch piece cinnamon stick

*Garnish*
5ml / 1 tsp *garam masala*
100ml / 3½fl oz plain yoghurt
30ml / 2 tbsp chopped fresh coriander
    leaves

Cook the potatoes in their skins in a little boiling, salted water for 10 minutes.
Drain well and prick all over with a skewer.
Heat the oil in a saucepan and let the cloves, bay leaf and cardamom begin to swell
before adding the turmeric and salt. Stir in a paste made by working the onion,
garlic, ginger and seeded chilli peppers with the lemon juice in a blender or food
processor. Simmer for about 10 minutes.
Add 50ml / 2fl oz water, the cinnamon and the potatoes and cook, tightly
covered, for another 10 minutes. Just before serving, top with the *garam masala*,
yoghurt and coriander.

# 'Hot' Aubergine Curry
## *Kathrikai Kara Kuzhambu*

This spicy vegetable dish comes from Madras. I find it effective to serve in small
quantities, rather like a pickle. If the finished dish is too hot for your taste, you can
always stir in a few tablespoons of plain yoghurt.

600g / 1lb 5oz aubergines (eggplants)
salt
125g / 4oz peeled tomatoes
1 large onion
4 large cloves garlic
60ml / 4 tbsp vegetable oil
15ml / 1 tbsp fenugreek seeds
15ml / 1 tbsp fennel seeds

15ml / 1 tbsp white or green mung
    beans (*moong dal*)
4 fresh or dried curry leaves
15ml / 1 tbsp chilli powder
30ml / 2 tbsp ground coriander
15 ml / 1 tbsp turmeric
25g / 1oz tamarind pulp (see page 13)

Cut the aubergines (eggplants) into small cubes, sprinkle with salt and leave for at
least an hour to 'purge'. Chop the tomatoes, onion and garlic. Heat the oil and
add the fenugreek and fennel seeds. When they have started to crackle, add the
onion, garlic, lentils and curry leaves. As soon as the onions start to change colour
add the ground spices, tomatoes and tamarind. Rinse the aubergines (eggplant)
and pat dry. Add them to the pan and cook gently until tender, being careful that
they do not over-cook and lose their shape. This dish can be served hot or cold.

# Vegetables & Lentils from Gujarat
## *Gujarati Dal*

This lovely vegetarian dish comes from Ahmedabad, the capital of Gujarat, the bastion of the Jain community which does not eat meat. They have created many subtly spiced vegetable stews. Gandhi established his Ashram just north of Ahmedabad, which saw the start of India's freedom movement.
If all the varieties of dal called for here are not available, make up the quantity with those to hand. A little chopped onion or garlic may be added if desired, but this does not appear in the authentic version.

50g / 2oz (¼ cup) *channa dal*
50g / 2oz (¼ cup) *masar dal*
50g / 2oz (¼ cup) mung beans (*moong dal*)
50g / 2oz (¼ cup) *toovar dal*
250g / 8oz peeled tomatoes
200g / 7oz courgettes (zucchini)
200g / 7oz aubergine (eggplant)
200g / 7oz sweet peppers
2 fresh hot green chilli peppers

30ml / 2 tbsp chopped fresh root ginger
5ml / 1 tsp turmeric
45ml / 3 tbsp vegetable oil
5ml / 1 tsp black mustard seeds
5ml / 1 tsp cumin seeds
2.5ml / ½ tsp asafoetida (optional)
15ml / 1 tbsp lemon juice
salt
30ml / 2 tbsp chopped fresh coriander leaves

Wash the dal and put to soak in water to cover for several hours. Chop the tomatoes, and cut the other vegetables into thick strips. Put the drained lentils into a pan with the seeded chilli peppers, ginger, turmeric and 750ml / 1¼ pints (3 cups) water. Simmer until tender. Cool and purée the mixture.
Heat the oil and add the mustard seeds, covering the pan to avoid the seeds popping out. After a few seconds add the cumin seeds, asafoetida and the vegetables. Cook for a few minutes, then stir in the lentil mixture. Simmer gently until the vegetables are cooked but not mushy.
Add the lemon juice and salt to taste and sprinkle with the chopped coriander.
This dish tastes just as good heated up the following day.

# Spinach & Lentil Purée
## *Keerai Massial*

This delicate vegetable dish comes from the Chettinad restaurant, Rain Tree in Madras. It makes a soothing contrast to some of the more fiery dishes.

500g / 1lb 2oz fresh spinach
100g / 3½oz green gram lentils (*moong dal*)
1 large onion
4 cloves garlic
2 fresh hot green chilli peppers
30ml / 2 tbsp vegetable oil
15ml / 1 tbsp cumin seeds
salt
25g / 1oz (2 tbsp) butter

Clean the lentils and cook in 250ml / 8fl oz water until soft but not pulped
Chop the onion, garlic and seeded chilli peppers. Heat the oil and add the cumin
seeds. When they begin to crackle in the oil, add the onion, garlic and chilli
peppers and cook until the onion is soft. Add the roughly chopped spinach and
cook over a gentle heat until wilted. Add the lentils and mash all the ingredients
together.
Let the mixture stand for a short while so that all the flavours amalgamate. Just
before serving, add salt to taste and pour the melted butter over.

# Punjab Five Jewels
## *Punj Rattani Dal*

This delicacy from the Punjab traditionally uses five different types of dal but it can be made with any combination of lentils and dried bean and peas, or even from only one variety.

50g / 2oz (¼ cup) mung beans (*moong dal*)
50g / 2oz (¼ cup) white gram beans (*urad dal*)
50g / 2oz (¼ cup) pink lentils (*masoor dal*)
5og / 2oz (¼ cup) yellow lentils (*toovar dal*)
50g / 2pz (¼ cup) yellow split peas (*channa dal*)
1 large onion
4 cloves garlic
3cm / 1¼ inch piece fresh root ginger
2 fresh hot green chilli peppers
30ml / 2 tbsp vegetable oil
5ml / 1 tsp turmeric
10ml / 2 tsp ground coriander
2.5ml / ½ tsp cayenne pepper
5ml / 1 tsp ground cumin
salt
30g / 1¼oz (2 tbsp) butter
2 peeled chopped tomatoes
5ml / 1 tsp *garam masala*
100ml / 3fl oz plain yoghurt
30ml / 2 tbsp chopped fresh coriander

Make a paste from the onion, garlic, ginger and seeded chilli peppers. Heat the oil and cook the paste for 5 minutes. Stir in the dal and when they are all coated with the mixture pour in 2 litres / 3½ pints (2 quarts) water. Bring to the boil and stir in the turmeric, coriander powder and cayenne pepper. Simmer until the dal are cooked and about half the liquid has evaporated. Sprinkle with the ground cumin and salt to taste.
Melt the butter in another pan and add the tomatoes, *garam masala* and yoghurt. Cook for about 10 minutes, then pour over the dal mixture and garnish with fresh coriander.

# Stuffed Pumpkin or Marrow
## *Kaddu*

1 small pumpkin or medium size vegetable marrow, weighing about
  1.5kg / 3½lb
salt
15ml / 1 tbsp vegetable oil
5ml / 1 tsp mustard seeds
1 large onion
4 cloves garlic
2 fresh hot green chilli peppers
5ml / 1 tsp ground cumin
10ml / 2 tsp ground coriander
2.5ml / 2 tsp turmeric
200g / 7oz (1½–2 cups) mixed vegetables such as peas, beans etc
30ml / 2 tbsp chopped fresh coriander leaves

*Sauce*
15ml / 1 tbsp vegetable oil
2 cloves garlic
1 medium onion
250g / 9oz (1¼ cups) peeled chopped tomatoes
200ml / 7fl oz plain yoghurt

Cut the pumpkin or marrow in half and scoop out the seeds and fibres. Sprinkle
with salt. Heat the oil and let the mustard seeds begin to pop before adding the
chopped onion, garlic and seeded chilli peppers. Add the spices and then the
vegetables. Add salt to taste and a little water. Cook the vegetables until they are
tender. The mixture should be rather dry.
Then use to stuff the pumpkin or marrow halves. Cover with foil and bake in a
preheated oven at 200°C / 400°F / gas 6 for 1 hour.
Make the sauce by heating the oil and cooking the chopped garlic and onion until
they are soft. Add the tomatoes and after 5 minutes the yoghurt. Add salt to taste.
Pour the sauce over the stuffed pumpkin or marrow and sprinkle with chopped
fresh coriander.

# Cauliflower
### *Gobi Masala*

**1 large cauliflower**
**15ml / 1 tbsp vegetable oil**
**5ml / 1 tsp black mustard seeds**
**5ml / 1 tsp ground coriander**
**5ml / 1 tsp cayenne pepper**
**5ml / 1 tsp turmeric**
**30ml / 2 tbsp chickpea flour (*besan*)**
**120g / 4oz (½ cup) creamed coconut dissolved in**
**200ml / 7fl oz boiling water**
**salt**
**15ml / 1 tbsp chopped fresh coriander leaves**

Cut the cauliflower into florets. Heat the oil and let the mustard seeds pop before adding the cauliflower. Stir for a few minutes before adding a paste made from the other ingredients, except the coriander. Cover and cook gently until the cauliflower is barely tender. Do not let it become too soft. Sprinkle with the coriander and serve.

# Sweetcorn
### *Makai*

**300g / 10oz (2 cups) sweetcorn kernels off the cob**
**15ml / 1 tbsp vegetable oil**
**1 large onion**
**3 fresh hot chilli peppers**
**5ml / 1 tsp ground coriander**
**5ml / 1 tsp ground cumin**
**200ml / 7fl oz plain yoghurt**
**salt**
**100ml / 3½fl oz cream**
**2.5ml / ½ tsp cayenne pepper**

Heat the oil and cook the finely chopped onion until it is soft. Seed the chilli peppers and slice into fine rounds. Add to the onion with the coriander and cumin and, after a few moments, stir in the sweetcorn. Mix 15ml / 1 tbsp water with the yoghurt and stir into the pan. Add a little salt. When the sweetcorn is tender, stir in the cream and sprinkle with cayenne pepper. Serve hot.

# Fish & Shellfish

FISHERMEN AT KOVALUM                    R BUDWIG

Years ago in Kovalem on the morning of New Year's Eve, I ventured out in one of the frail, local dug-out boats. Our boatman bought a lobster and some mussels from one of the neighbouring fishing boats, and we landed on a deserted beach and made a fire on some rocks. We quenched our thirst with coconuts from the overhead trees while he cooked our purchases without the benefit of any spices or salt. The taste was so good, and I always think of this whenever I eat fish in India. The long coastline and rivers of India provide a myriad of fish, and at Madras fish market I saw a bewildering selection, including baby shark. Every region has its own speciality, and I made a collection of recipes for prawn curry, every one a different colour because of the local variation in spices.

# Goan Clams
*Teesryo*

This is a simple fish dish from Goa. In India it is usually made with small cockles, but I prefer to use clams.

1kg / 2¼lb clams
45ml / 3 tbsp vegetable oil
4 cloves garlic
4cm / 1½ inch piece fresh root ginger
1 large onion
2 fresh hot green chilli peppers
10ml / 2 tsp turmeric
30ml / 2 tbsp ground coriander
5ml / 1 tsp cayenne pepper
salt
100g / 3½oz (1 cup) freshly grated coconut
15ml / 1 tbsp lemon juice
15ml / 1 tbsp chopped fresh coriander leaves

Heat the oil and fry the chopped garlic, ginger, onion and seeded chilli peppers until the onion is golden brown. Stir in the turmeric, ground coriander and cayenne pepper and, after a few minutes, add the clams with salt to taste. Simmer, covered, for about 10 minutes, by which time the shells should have opened. Remove from the heat and put in a serving bowl. Sprinkle with the freshly grated coconut, the lemon juice and fresh coriander, and serve.

# Tandoori Lobster

A simple but delicious way to serve lobster.

2 raw lobsters
6 cloves garlic
5cm / 2 inch piece fresh root ginger
30ml / 2 tbsp lemon juice
150ml / 5fl oz cream
50g / 2oz (½ cup) chickpea flour (*besan*)
1 egg
25ml / 5 tsp carom
10ml / 2 tsp *garam masala*
5ml / 1 tsp pepper
5ml / 1 tsp salt
40g / 1½oz (3 tbsp) butter for basting the lobsters

Cut the lobsters in half lengthways and remove the vein. Take the meat from the shell. Wash and dry the shell and set aside. Make a paste of the other ingredients, except the butter. Rub the lobster meat with paste and leave to marinate for 5–6 hours. Put the meat back in the shells and dot with the butter. Roast in a preheated oven at 180°C / 350°F / gas 4 for 15 minutes.

# Kerala Prawns in Coconut Milk
*Verra Moolee*

A recipe from the beautiful, palm-fringed coast of Kerala.

1kg / 2¼lb large raw prawns (shrimp) in shell
100ml / 3½fl oz vegetable oil
1 large onion
4 cloves garlic
4cm / 1½ inch piece fresh root ginger
4 fresh hot green chilli peppers
30ml / 2 tbsp ground coriander
5ml / 1 tsp turmeric
500ml / 16fl oz coconut 'milk' (see page 14)
salt
30g / 1¼oz (⅔ cup) fresh coriander leaves

Heat the oil and fry the finely chopped onion until golden brown. Very finely chop the garlic, ginger and seeded chilli peppers and cook with the onions for about 5 minutes. Stir in the spices and after a few seconds pour in the coconut milk. Simmer for up to 15 minutes, until reduced, then add salt to taste. Shell the prawns (shrimp), remove the vein down the back and pat dry. Cook them gently in the spiced coconut sauce for about 10 minutes. Just before serving, stir in the chopped coriander leaves.

# Fish in Tomato Sauce
*Machi Hazur Pasand*

This simple, delicate fish dish has become a firm favourite even with my most conservative friends.

1 white fish fillet, weighing 1kg / 2½lb
25g / 1oz (2 tbsp) *ghee* or butter
5ml / 1 tsp ground fenugreek
4 cloves garlic
4cm / 1½ inch piece fresh root ginger
15ml / 1 tbsp ground coriander
15ml / 1 tbsp ground cumin

5ml / 1 tsp turmeric
400g / 14oz tin tomatoes
5ml / 1 tsp paprika
60ml / 4 tbsp cream
250ml / 8fl oz plain yoghurt
1.25ml / ¼ tsp cayenne pepper
2.5ml / ½ tsp salt
vinegar

Heat the *ghee* or butter and fry the fenugreek and finely chopped garlic and ginger. When they are golden brown, add the coriander, cumin, turmeric and tomatoes. Stir in the paprika, cream, yoghurt and about 350ml / 12fl oz of water. Bring to the boil and simmer until reduced by half. Work in a food processor or blender to make a smooth sauce.
Put the fish in a long baking dish and dust with the cayenne and salt. Sprinkle with the vinegar and put in a 200°C / 400°F / gas 6 oven until the vinegar has evaporated. Pour the sauce over the fish, reduce the oven heat to 180°C / 350°F / gas 4 and cook for a further 30 minutes. Garnish the fish with thin lemon slices and return to the oven to cook for another 7 minutes. Serve hot.

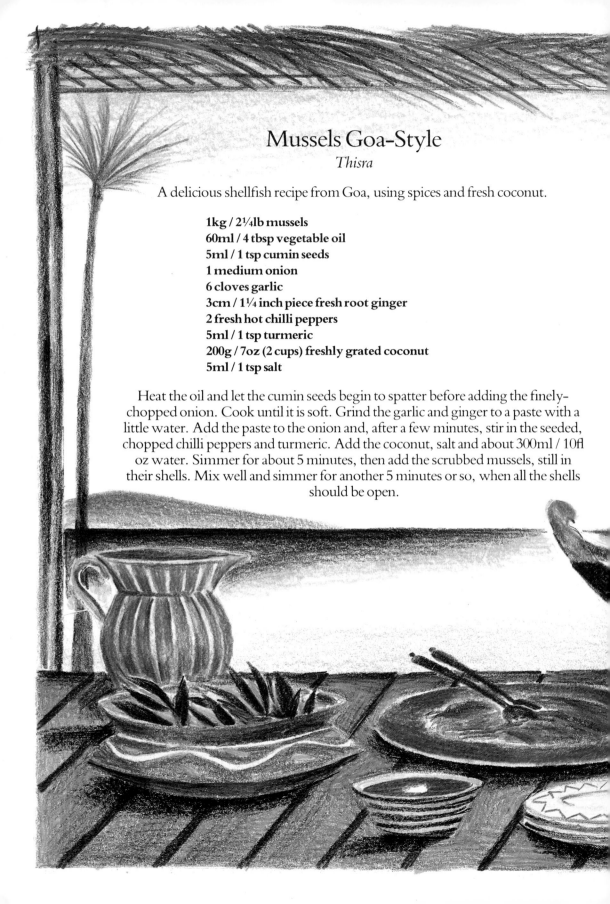

# Mussels Goa-Style
## *Thisra*

A delicious shellfish recipe from Goa, using spices and fresh coconut.

**1kg / 2¼lb mussels**
**60ml / 4 tbsp vegetable oil**
**5ml / 1 tsp cumin seeds**
**1 medium onion**
**6 cloves garlic**
**3cm / 1¼ inch piece fresh root ginger**
**2 fresh hot chilli peppers**
**5ml / 1 tsp turmeric**
**200g / 7oz (2 cups) freshly grated coconut**
**5ml / 1 tsp salt**

Heat the oil and let the cumin seeds begin to spatter before adding the finely-chopped onion. Cook until it is soft. Grind the garlic and ginger to a paste with a little water. Add the paste to the onion and, after a few minutes, stir in the seeded, chopped chilli peppers and turmeric. Add the coconut, salt and about 300ml / 10fl oz water. Simmer for about 5 minutes, then add the scrubbed mussels, still in their shells. Mix well and simmer for another 5 minutes or so, when all the shells should be open.

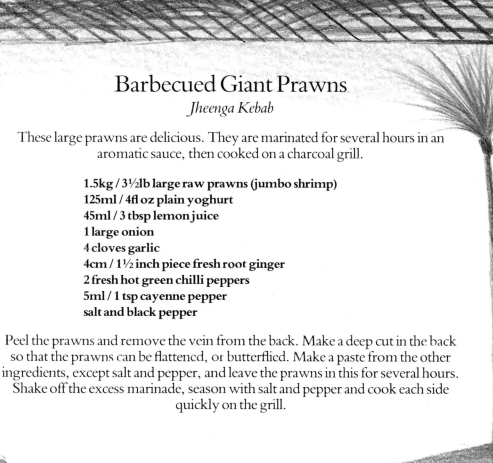

# Barbecued Giant Prawns
### *Jheenga Kebab*

These large prawns are delicious. They are marinated for several hours in an aromatic sauce, then cooked on a charcoal grill.

**1.5kg / 3½lb large raw prawns (jumbo shrimp)**
**125ml / 4fl oz plain yoghurt**
**45ml / 3 tbsp lemon juice**
**1 large onion**
**4 cloves garlic**
**4cm / 1½ inch piece fresh root ginger**
**2 fresh hot green chilli peppers**
**5ml / 1 tsp cayenne pepper**
**salt and black pepper**

Peel the prawns and remove the vein from the back. Make a deep cut in the back so that the prawns can be flattened, or butterflied. Make a paste from the other ingredients, except salt and pepper, and leave the prawns in this for several hours. Shake off the excess marinade, season with salt and pepper and cook each side quickly on the grill.

# Parsi Fish Parcels
*Patrani Machi*

This light, delicate Parsi dish is traditionally prepared with stuffed fillets of pomfret steamed in banana leaves. I have tried several ways of getting a similar effect, and my favourite version wraps the fish in large spinach leaves and in foil. When the foil is removed the fragrant green parcels look extremely elegant, and I often serve them as a main course with European food for a dinner party.

6 white fish fillets
salt
90ml / 6 tbsp white wine vinegar
6 large green leaves, spinach or chard
4 fresh hot green chilli peppers
100g / 3½oz (1 cup) freshly grated coconut
50g / 2oz (1 cup) fresh coriander leaves

4 cloves garlic
15ml / 1 tbsp coriander seeds
15ml / 1 tbsp cumin seeds
5ml / 1 tsp cayenne pepper
15ml / 1 tbsp sugar
60ml / 4 tbsp lemon juice
Thin slices of lemon to garnish

Wash and dry the fish fillets and sprinkle them with salt and the vinegar. Leave to marinate for an hour. If the fillets are thick enough, make some horizontal slits to create little pockets. Plunge the spinach leaves in boiling water, drain carefully, pat dry and set aside. Remove the seeds from the chilli peppers and put them with the remaining ingredients into the food processor. Work to form a smooth paste. Dry the fish and spread each side thickly with the paste. If you have been able to make pockets, force the paste inside them. Roll up each fillet inside a spinach leaf and then wrap tightly in foil. Cook in a steamer or in a baking dish in a 180°C / 350°F / gas 4 oven, for about 25 minutes. Remove the foil, and garnish with lemon slices.

# Barbecued Skewers of Fish

*Seekh Ki Machali*

I first tried this sitting by a charcoal brazier in the gardens of Delhi's Taj Majal Hotel while the chilly night air was filled with the sound of an American Marine Band playing the music of Glenn Miller. The surprising combination added extra spice to the dish, but it tasted just as good when I made it at home without the music.

500g / 1lb 2oz firm white fish
5ml / 1 tsp salt
6 cloves of garlic
4cm / 1½ inch piece fresh root ginger
15ml / 1 tbsp *garam masala*
15ml / 1 tbsp ground coriander
5ml / 1 tsp cayenne pepper
150ml / 4fl oz plain yoghurt
15ml / 1 tbsp vegetable oil
1 lemon
2 fresh hot green chilli peppers

Fillet and skin the fish, then cut into 4cm / 1½ inch cubes. Put about five pieces on each skewer and sprinkle with the salt. Make a paste from the garlic, ginger, spices and yoghurt and use to cover the fish. Leave for a few hours, then grill. The skewers can be sprinkled with a little oil during cooking, if required. Garnish with the lemon cut into wedges and fine rings of seeded green chilli pepper.

# Goan Fish Curry
## *Goan Machi*

All along the Konkan coast, a variety of fish and shellfish are cooked in a hot sweet and sour coconut sauce. 'Kokum' fruit is used with tamarind to produce a sour effect, but the curry can be made successfully with limes or lemons as a replacement. I find the flavour improved if the fish is prepared a day in advance.

750g / 1¾lb firm white fish fillets
5ml / 1 tsp turmeric
salt
30ml / 2 tsp lemon juice
3 dried hot red chilli peppers
5ml / 1 tsp cumin seed
30ml / 2 tbsp coriander seeds
5ml / 1 tsp black peppercorns
6 cloves garlic
3cm / 1¼ inch piece peeled fresh root ginger
250g / 9oz (2½ cups) freshly grated coconut
1 large onion
30ml / 2 tbsp vegetable oil
150ml / 5fl oz tamarind juice (see page 13)
5 *kokums* or chopped flesh from ½ lime or lemon
200g / 7oz peeled tomatoes
3 fresh hot green chilli peppers

Sprinkle the fish fillets with the turmeric, a little salt and the lemon juice. Leave for several hours.
Grind the seeded red chilli peppers, cumin and coriander seeds and peppercorns to a fine powder, then work with the garlic, ginger and coconut in a food processor to form a smooth paste. Chop the onion and fry in the heated oil until golden brown. Add the spice paste and cook gently for 10 minutes. Pour in 1 litre/1¼ pints (1 quart) of boiling water and simmer for 20 minutes.
Now put in the fish and its liquid, together with the tamarind juice and the *kokums*. Cook gently for 10 minutes. Just at the very end, add the chopped tomatoes and seeded green chilli peppers.

# Poultry

*A*lthough ducks, geese, partridge and quail are all quite common in Indian cooking, chicken is the most popular bird. In the past, chickens were very expensive and reserved for feasts and special occasions. Today with large-scale farming, they have become more affordable, but chicken dishes are still regarded as rather special.

Tandoori chicken, originally from the North West frontier, has become a universal favourite, but it can only be made really well in a traditional Tandoor oven, where the clay lends its own smokey flavour. For westerners who want to achieve a quick approximation, various ready-made spice mixtures are available on the market with instructions for marinating and oven cooking. Here, however, I have concentrated on favourite chicken recipes which can be a total success for the international cook.

# Chicken with Apricots
## *Murgh Khumani*

The Parsis fled their native Persia over a thousand years ago to escape persecution for their Zoroastrian religion. They settled in Gujarat and Bombay and, to honour the Hindu Raja of Sanjan who first granted them asylum, they vowed never to eat beef. They still maintain this promise, but it has in no way inhibited their lavish meals – it has been said that Parsis can be divided into two groups, those who love good food and those who love eating. Two great Parsi chefs, Cyrus Elavia and Cyrus Todiwala, have taught me various specialities, including this chicken and apricot dish which often appears as one of the many delights at local wedding feasts.

**1 chicken or chicken pieces weighing 1.5kg / 3½lb**
**120g / 4oz dried apricots**
**6 cloves**
**6 whole green cardamom pods**
**4cm / 1½ inch stick cinnamon**
**10ml / 2 tsp cumin seeds**
**2 cloves garlic**
**2cm / ¾inch square fresh root ginger**
**10ml / 2 tsp salt**
**30ml / 2 tbsp vegetable oil**
**3 medium onions**
**4 fresh hot green chilli peppers**
**1 large red ripe tomato or 20ml / 4 tsp tomato paste**
**10ml / 2 tsp sugar**
**30ml / 2 tbsp white wine vinegar**

Skin the chicken and, if whole, divide into eight portions. Grind the spices, and finely chop the garlic and ginger. Cook the apricots in 300ml / 10fl oz water until they are soft but still firm. Rub the chicken with the salt and half the spices, garlic and ginger. Leave in a cool place for several hours.
Heat the oil and fry the finely sliced onions until they are golden brown. Stir in the seeded and finely chopped chilli peppers, the remaining spices, ginger and garlic, then add the chicken pieces, turning them over so that each side is coloured. Stir in the chopped tomato or tomato paste and a little water and simmer over a low heat for about 30 minutes. Add the sugar and vinegar and cook for another 15 minutes.
Gently stir in the apricots with their liquid and leave for at least an hour so that the flavours can amalgamate. Reheat before serving.
This dish is usually served topped with straw potatoes (*sali*) – see page 88 – but I prefer to serve it with fragrant rice.

# Saffron & Almond Chicken Breast
## *Murgh Wajid Ali*

Lucknow's last ruler, Wajid Ali Shah, was a legend for his heady excesses. His extravagant court echoed with plaintive love songs, '*ghazels*', and the dancing girls were known for their culture and wit. He was a great gourmet and this elaborate party dish is named after him.

**6 chicken breast fillets (skinless, boneless chicken breast halves)**
**slivered almonds, to garnish**

*Marinade*
**3 cloves garlic**
**2cm / ¾ inch piece fresh root ginger**
**5ml / 1 tsp *garam masala***
**5ml / 1 tsp salt**
**2.5ml / ½ tsp paprika**
**15ml / 3 tsp vegetable oil**

*Filling*
**4 fresh hot green chilli peppers**
**1 large onion**
**4cm / 1½ inch piece fresh root ginger**
**30ml / 2 tbsp fresh coriander leaves**
**30ml / 2 tbsp lemon juice**
**5ml / 1 tsp salt**
**100g / 3½oz (½ cup) ricotta or cottage cheese**

*Sauce*

| | |
|---|---|
| **50g / 2oz (⅓ cup) shelled cashew nuts** | **1 small onion** |
| **15ml / 1 tbsp desiccated (dried shredded) coconut** | **200ml / 7fl oz plain yoghurt** |
| | **salt** |
| **2 cloves garlic** | **5ml / 1 tsp *garam masala*** |
| **2cm / ¾ inch piece fresh root ginger** | **5ml / 1 tsp saffron threads** |
| **30ml / 2 tbsp vegetable oil** | |

Very finely chop the ginger and garlic and mix with the other marinade ingredients. Rub the chicken breasts with the mixture and leave for an hour. Seed the chilli peppers and put in the food processor with the remaining filling ingredients. Work to a paste.

For the sauce, work the cashew nuts and coconut with 100ml / 3½fl oz water to a paste. Make a paste with the garlic, ginger and 5ml / 1 tsp water. Heat the oil and cook the finely chopped onion until it is soft. Add the ginger and garlic paste and, when it is dry, stir in the cashew paste. Simmer for 5 minutes, then add the yoghurt, salt to taste, *garam masala* and saffron dissolved in a little warm milk. Set aside and keep warm.

Carefully stuff the chicken fillets by placing a portion of filling on each and rolling the chicken around it. Place the fillets on a greased baking tray, with the seam underneath. Cover with foil and roast in a preheated oven at 180°C / 350°F / gas 4 for 15 minutes to let the chicken get slightly brown. Carefully transfer to a serving dish and spoon over the sauce. Garnish with slivered almonds.

# Kashmiri Duck

*Batak Kashmiri*

Every race that has ruled India over the centuries has seen Kashmir as an earthly paradise. The great Moghul Jahangir, whose name means 'seizer of the world', when asked for his dying wish, murmured, 'Kashmir, only Kashmir.' Later rulers gloried in the game to be found in the mountains and lakes. This recipe combines the local wild duck with walnuts and cherries. It is an interesting variation on the popular duck with orange sauce, and there are no 'hot' spices.

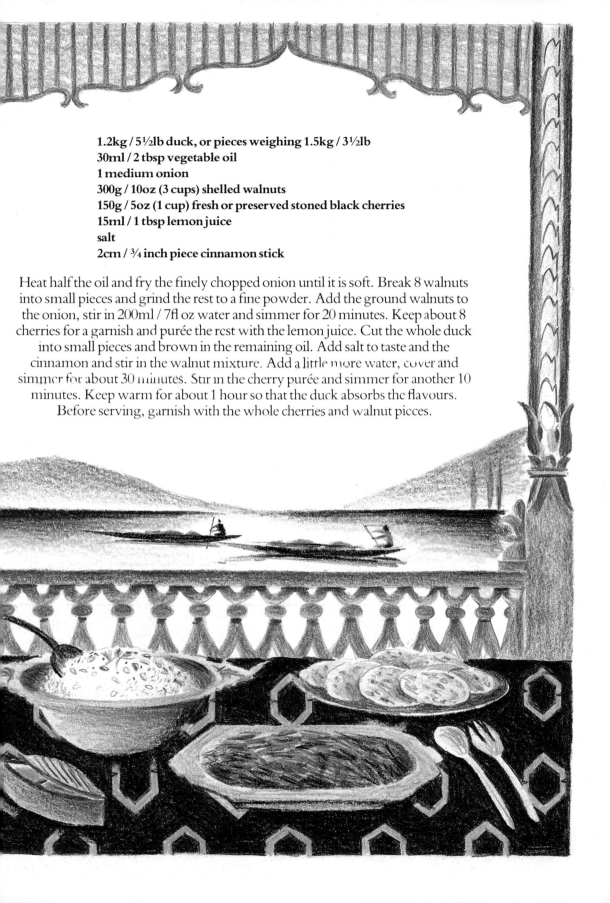

**1.2kg / 5½lb duck, or pieces weighing 1.5kg / 3½lb**
**30ml / 2 tbsp vegetable oil**
**1 medium onion**
**300g / 10oz (3 cups) shelled walnuts**
**150g / 5oz (1 cup) fresh or preserved stoned black cherries**
**15ml / 1 tbsp lemon juice**
**salt**
**2cm / ¾ inch piece cinnamon stick**

Heat half the oil and fry the finely chopped onion until it is soft. Break 8 walnuts into small pieces and grind the rest to a fine powder. Add the ground walnuts to the onion, stir in 200ml / 7fl oz water and simmer for 20 minutes. Keep about 8 cherries for a garnish and purée the rest with the lemon juice. Cut the whole duck into small pieces and brown in the remaining oil. Add salt to taste and the cinnamon and stir in the walnut mixture. Add a little more water, cover and simmer for about 30 minutes. Stir in the cherry purée and simmer for another 10 minutes. Keep warm for about 1 hour so that the duck absorbs the flavours. Before serving, garnish with the whole cherries and walnut pieces.

# Duck with Cashew Nuts
## *Vath*

In Kerala there is a small community known as Syrian Christians. Around the year 52 AD, the Apostle Thomas Didymus is thought to have travelled to Kerala and converted some of the local people to Christianity. Many years later their numbers increased when another Thomas led a small group from Syria to escape religious persecution. Thomas of Canaan became adviser to the local ruler who, at court banquets, as a mark of great honour, had Thomas's food served on a double banana leaf. Even today the Syrian Christians fold over their banana leaves to honour Thomas's memory. The inland waterways attract wild ducks and this recipe is a speciality from the nearby town of Alleppey.

**1.2kg / 5½lb duck**

**Stuffing**
**50g / 2oz (⅔ cup) dried breadcrumbs**
**15ml / 1 tbsp raisins**
**15ml / 1 tbsp chopped fresh coriander leaves**
**10ml / 2 tsp sugar**
**15ml / 1 tbsp vinegar**
**5ml / 1 salt**
**5ml / 1 tsp black pepper**
**15ml / 1 tbsp vegetable oil**
**1 small onion**

**3 cloves garlic**
**2cm / ¾ inch piece fresh root ginger**
**5ml / 1 tsp ground cumin**
**5ml / 1 tsp turmeric**
**liver and heart from duck**
**200g / 7oz (1 cup) peeled, chopped tomatoes**
**8 whole green cardamom pods**
**1 fresh hot green chilli pepper**
**80g / 1oz (⅔ cup) shelled cashew nuts**
**2.5ml / ½ tsp cayenne pepper**
**2 hard boiled eggs**

Mix together breadcrumbs, raisins, coriander, sugar, vinegar, salt, pepper. Heat the oil and add the finely chopped onion, garlic and ginger. When the onion is golden brown, stir in the cumin, turmeric and minced (ground) duck liver and heart. When the offal begins to brown, add the tomatoes and the ground seeds from the cardamom pods. Finely slice the green chilli pepper, keeping the seeds intact unless you want a mild dish. Stir into the stuffing and add the chopped cashew nuts and cayenne pepper. Cut the eggs lengthways into quarters and place them gently in the stuffing mixture.

Dry the duck and prick the skin all over. Rub with salt and stuff from the neck end. Sew up the cavity. Place the duck on one side in a roasting tin in a preheated oven at 230°C / 450°F / gas 8. After 15 minutes, turn the duck on to its other side. Now turn the oven down to 180°C / 350°F / gas 4 and roast, breast up, for another hour and a half. From time to time, baste the bird with the drippings in the tin.

# Stuffed Chicken Breasts

*Shaan-e-Murgh*

This is a delicious sort of Indian Chicken Kiev.

**6 chicken breast fillets with wing bone intact**
**vegetable oil for deep frying**

*Marinade*
**2 cloves garlic**
**2cm / ¾ inch piece fresh root ginger**
**60ml / 4 tbsp lemon juice**
**2.5ml / ½ tsp cayenne pepper**
**salt**

| *Stuffing* | *Batter* |
|---|---|
| **20g / ⅔oz (½ cup) fresh coriander leaves** | **200g / 7oz (1½ cups) flour** |
| **6 fresh hot green chilli peppers** | **salt** |
| **40g / 1½oz (¼ cup) shelled cashew nuts** | **3 eggs** |
| **2 rings of fresh pineapple** | |
| **200g / 7oz *paneer*, ricotta or cottage cheese** | |
| **5ml / 1 tsp black cumin seeds** | |
| **salt** | |

For the marinade, finely chop the garlic with the ginger and mix with the other marinade ingredients. Rub the chicken with the marinade and leave for an hour.

For the stuffing, chop the coriander, seeded chilli peppers, cashew nuts and pineapple into small pieces and stir into the mashed cheese. Add the cumin and salt. Spoon a portion of the stuffing on to the middle of each chicken fillet and roll the meat over to form a parcel with the bone sticking out. Chill the stuffed breasts for at least 30 minutes, or until you are ready to fry them.

Make a thick batter. Heat the oil in a deep pan to 190°C / 375°F. Dip each stuffed chicken breast into the batter, then put it into the hot oil. Unless you have a very large pan, fry only two breasts at a time until they are golden brown on all sides. Keep them warm in the oven until all are fried.

# Nine Jewelled Chicken

## *Murgh Navrattan*

A special occasion dish, this always draws admiration. Akbar, the greatest of the Moghul emperors, combined outstanding physical prowess and zest for life with a liberal love of the arts which flourished in his long reign. In an age of zealots (the late sixteenth century), he showed great religious tolerance, and with the help of his enlightened ministers he tried to improve the lot of his countrymen. This recipe pays tribute to Akbar's 'nine jewels', his noble counsellors.

8 small skinned chicken portions
350ml / 12fl oz plain yoghurt
salt
2 medium onions
5ml / 1 tbsp chopped fresh root ginger
4 fresh hot green chilli peppers
40g / 1½oz (¼ cup) blanched almonds
40g / 1½oz (¼ cup) shelled cashew nuts
30ml / 2 tbsp white poppy seeds
30ml / 2 tbsp vegetable oil

6 whole green cardamom pods
5 cloves
4cm / 1½ inch stick cinnamon
1 bay leaf
2.5ml / ½ tsp turmeric
10ml / 2 tsp cayenne pepper
125ml / 4fl oz cream
5ml / 1 tsp ground mace
5ml / 1 tsp ground green cardamom

*Nine Jewels for garnishing*
15 blanched pistachio nuts
20 slivered almonds
10 shelled cashew nuts
10 walnut halves
10 pine nuts

15 raisins
15 sultanas (golden raisins)
threads of lemon rind
threads of orange rind

Put the chicken portions to marinate in the yoghurt with a little salt. Chop the onions, ginger and seeded chilli peppers. Grind the nuts and poppy seeds with a little water to make a smooth paste. Heat the oil, add the whole spices and bay leaf and when they begin to crackle add the chopped onions. Cook until golden brown, then add the ginger, chilli peppers, turmeric and cayenne pepper. Stir for a few minutes, then add the chicken with its liquid and about 150ml / 5fl oz water. Cook until the chicken is tender. Now stir in the poppy paste, the cream, mace and ground cardamom. Taste for salt. Serve arranged on a shallow dish, decorated with the 'nine jewels'.

# Chettinad Chicken Pepper Fry
## *Kozhi Melagu Varuval*

In Southern India the Chettiar community became a tribe of thrifty merchant bankers, travelling through all of South East Asia earning a good living. On their return they brought home slightly different eating habits, and in the largely vegetarian South this robust, spicy, non-vegetarian food was regarded as food for warriors. Eating houses known as Military Hotels appeared, catering for regulars and visitors wanting to sample Chettinad cooking.

In Madras, 'The Rain Tree' restaurant, which must be the most beautiful open-air restaurant in India, specialises in Chettinad cooking. The tables are grouped around an ancient Rain Tree, and the enchanted garden is lit as skilfully as a stage set. The marvellous food is served on banana leaves and a solitary figure, dressed in white, plays strange melodies on a simple reed pipe. This is a very 'hot' dish from 'The Rain Tree'.

1 chicken
30ml / 2 tbsp vegetable oil
2 medium onions
2 cloves garlic
2cm / ¾ inch piece fresh root ginger
5ml / 1 tsp turmeric
5ml / 1 tsp cayenne pepper
5ml / 1 tsp ground coriander
6 fresh or dried curry leaves
50g / 2 oz crushed black peppercorns
150g / 5oz (¾ cup) peeled chopped tomatoes
salt

Cut the chicken into small pieces. Heat the oil and fry the finely chopped onions, garlic and ginger. When they begin to turn colour, add the spices and cook for a few minutes longer. Now add the tomatoes and salt to taste and cook for a further 5 minutes.

Put in the chicken pieces and stir so that they are thoroughly coated with the sauce. Cover and simmer for about 30 minutes. At the end of this time the mixture should be almost dry, but you need to check from time to time and add a little water if necessary.

# Cochin Chicken
## *Murgh Cochin*

Cochin in Kerala has been the centre of the spice trade since the beginning of time, and the inland waterways meander inevitably towards the good natural harbour. The population is made up of many races and the first Jews settled here in the first century after Christ to remove themselves from Roman jurisdiction. The historic Jew Town grew up around the small, simple synagogue, but today the Jewish community is dying out as most of the young people have emigrated to Israel. The community elder is Mr. S. Koder whose family came from Iraq two centuries ago and this is one of their specialities.

| | |
|---|---|
| 1 chicken or 8 chicken pieces, 1.5kg / 3½lb | 10 fresh hot green chilli peppers |
| 30ml / 2 tbsp vegetable oil | 225g / 8oz tin peeled tomatoes |
| 8 fresh or dried curry leaves | 5ml / 1 tsp turmeric |
| 250g / 9oz onions | 5ml / 1 tsp cayenne pepper |
| 6 cloves garlic | 5ml / 1 tsp black pepper |
| 4cm / 1½ inch piece fresh root ginger | 200ml / 7fl oz tamarind juice page 13 |
| | sugar, salt |

If using a whole chicken, divide it into eight portions. Remove the skin from the chicken. Heat the oil and add first the curry leaves and then the finely-chopped onions, garlic and ginger and seeded chilli peppers cut into thin rings. When the onion has changed colour add the chopped tomatoes, the turmeric, cayenne and black pepper. Put in the chicken pieces and add about 250ml / 8fl oz water. Cover and simmer gently for about half an hour.
Now stir in the strained tamarind infusion, sugar and salt and simmer for another 5 minutes. Before serving boil over a fierce heat so that the sauce reduces.

# Chicken Cardamom
## *Murgh Elaichi*

The delicate, perfumed spices in this dish from the North transform even a battery chicken into an exotic feast. There are no 'hot' spices.

| | |
|---|---|
| 1 large chicken | *Marinade* |
| 15ml / 1 tbsp vegetable oil | 12 whole green cardamom pods |
| 6 cloves | 5ml / 1 tsp fennel seeds |
| 3 cinnamon sticks 4cm / 1½ inches long | 3cm / 1¼ inch piece fresh root ginger |
| 1 large onion | 3 cloves garlic |
| 15ml / 1 tbsp milk | 250ml / 8fl oz plain yoghurt |
| 5ml / 1 tsp saffron threads | 5ml / 1 tsp cayenne pepper |
| | salt |

Grind the marinade spices, then work in a food processor with the ginger, garlic, yoghurt and cayenne pepper to make a thick paste. Rub the chicken with salt and make deep holes all over with a skewer. Rub the paste over the chicken and leave for several hours so that the spices can penetrate. It can be left, covered, in the refrigerator overnight, if desired.

Heat the oil and let the cloves and cinnamon swell before adding the finely chopped onion. Fry gently until it is golden brown. Shake any excess marinade off the chicken and brown it quickly in the oil on all sides. Warm the milk and dissolve the saffron in it. Put the chicken in an oven dish and pour over any remaining marinade and the saffron milk. Cover tightly with foil and cook in a preheated oven at 180°C / 350°F / gas 4 until the chicken is tender.

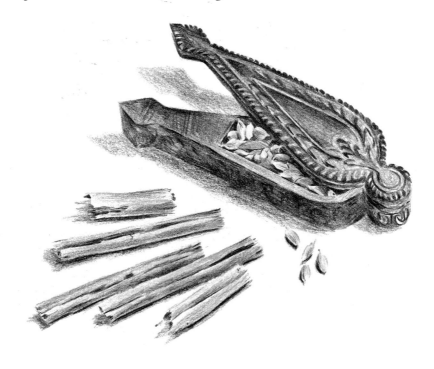

# Meat

$S$ince Hindus do not eat beef and Muslims do not eat pork, the most common meat eaten in India is 'mutton'. This so-called 'mutton' is, in fact, goat and only in the extreme north and Kashmir is real lamb served. The meat is usually rather tough so it is marinated in yoghurt or grated papaya to make it more tender. The Syrian Christians on the Malabar coast have some beef dishes and Goa has its famous pork 'vindaloo' and 'sorpotel'. During the days of the princes, game provided some variety, but today hunting is illegal in most regions.

For the following recipes that I have selected it is possible to use whichever meat you prefer since the spices are the most important flavour.

# Pork with Honey
## *Shikar Korma*

Hunting has always been a favourite pastime in India, and many miniatures depict lively groups of nobles on horseback pursuing their quarry. In Rajasthan, wild boar was enjoyed and this pork recipe carries the name of the hunt, *shikar*.

1kg / 2¼lb lean boneless pork
30ml / 2 tbsp honey
4 whole green cardamom pods
2cm / ¾ inch stick cinnamon
5ml / 1 tsp mace
5ml / 1 tsp turmeric
5ml / 1 tsp black pepper

3 small onions
2 cloves garlic
30ml / 2 tbsp vegetable oil
salt
15ml / 1 tbsp mixed grated orange
   and lemon rind
200ml / 7fl oz plain yoghurt
5ml / 1 tsp flour

Cut the pork into cubes. Grind the cardamom and cinnamon stick and mix with the ground spices. Finely chop the onions and garlic. Heat a heavy pan and warm the honey. Add the oil and when it is warm, stir in the pork. Cook until all the pieces are golden brown. Add 200ml / 7fl oz water and salt to taste. Simmer until tender, then turn up the heat so that all the liquid evaporates.

Add the garlic, onions, spices and citrus rind and cook gently for a few minutes. Gradually stir in the yoghurt beaten with the flour. Heat gently, then cover and remove from heat. Keep warm for about 25 minutes before serving so that the flavours amalgamate.

# Lamb with Yoghurt & Almonds
### *Safed Maas*

The Indian Kingdom of Rajasthan was famous for its fierce warriors and beautiful women, and the invading Moghuls, appreciating excellence in all forms, made close alliances with the Rajput princesses. This ancient Rajastani delicacy shows that the 'borrowing' was a two-way arrangement. Today, in Jodhpur, Rani Usha Devi has this dish served to her guests at Ajit Bhawan hotel, the courtyard lit with charcoal braziers glowing through filigree stone screens.

| | |
|---|---|
| 1kg / 2¼lb lean, boneless lamb | 6 whole green cardamom pods |
| 300ml / 10fl oz plain yoghurt | 30ml / 2 tbsp ground coriander |
| 30g / 1¼oz (3½ tbsp) blanched almonds | salt |
| 30ml / 2 tbsp chopped fresh root ginger | 5ml / 1 tsp white pepper |
| 2 medium onions | 120ml / 4fl oz cream, or additional plain yoghurt if preferred |

Cut the lamb into 2.5cm / 1 inch cubes. *Safed maas* means white meat, so the lamb is usually first blanched in boiling salted water for 5 minutes. Put the ginger, almonds, onions and yoghurt in a food processor and work to make a fine paste. Put this mixture into a heavy saucepan together with the lamb, crushed cardamom pods, coriander, salt to taste and pepper. Cover and cook very gently until the meat is tender. Stir in the cream and adjust the seasoning before serving. Do not allow to boil again.

# Lamb & Spinach
## *Palak Gosht*

In Indian cooking there are many delicious combinations of lamb and a leafy
green vegetable. In Hyderabad the Moghul tradition introduced lamb cooked
with sorrel, the subtle *gosht chuggar* and in the Punjab the pungent mustard greens
*sarson ka saag* give the lamb a more robust taste. This lamb and spinach dish is
simpler than the Moghul version and it pleases most palates.

800g / 1¾lb lean boneless lamb
500g / 1lb 2oz fresh spinach
2 onions
4 large cloves garlic
30ml / 2 tbsp finely chopped fresh root
    ginger
5 fresh hot green chilli peppers

60ml / 4 tbsp vegetable oil
5ml / 1 tsp black cumin seeds
4 whole green cardamom pods
5ml / 1 tsp black pepper
salt
250ml / 8fl oz plain yoghurt

Trim all fat from the lamb and cut it into cubes. Put the onions, garlic, ginger and
seeded chilli peppers into a food processor and work to make a smooth paste.
Heat the oil and put in the black cumin seeds. When the seeds begin to spatter add
the onion paste and fry for about 10 minutes. When the oil separates out from the
mixture, stir in the lamb cubes. Cover and cook over a low heat for about 10
minutes then remove the lid and let the meat juices evaporate.
Now add the chopped spinach, the crushed cardamom pods, pepper, and salt to
taste. Cover and cook slowly for about an hour, adding a little water if necessary.
Remove from the heat, stir in the yoghurt and serve.

# Lamb with Yoghurt & Fresh Coriander

*Dhaniawala Gosht*

This subtle, aromatic Moghul lamb dish is simple to prepare and contains no 'hot' ingredients. The meat is coated in an elegant pale yellow sauce, flecked with green.

1kg / 2¼lb lean boneless lamb, from the leg
1 litre / 1¾ pints (1 quart) thick, full-fat plain yoghurt
300g / 7oz (3½ cups) fresh coriander leaves
500ml / 16fl oz meat stock
5ml / 1 tsp turmeric
5ml / 1 tsp salt
30ml / 2 tbsp vegetable oil
4 cloves
4 whole green cardamom pods
4 black peppercorns
4cm / 1½ inch stick cinnamon
2 cloves garlic

Trim all fat from the lamb and cut it into 2.5cm / 1 inch cubes. Put it to cook in the boiling stock, together with the turmeric and salt. Simmer for about an hour. In a separate pan, heat the oil and add the whole spices. Once they have swelled, add the finely chopped garlic and the well-stirred yoghurt. Raise the heat and cook the yoghurt mixture, stirring from time to time, until it has reduced to a thick sauce. Discard the whole spices. Use a slotted spoon to lift the lamb from its liquid and stir it into the yoghurt sauce, making sure each piece is coated with the sauce. Now gradually add the strained lamb stock and simmer gently until the sauce is once more thick. Just before serving, stir in the finely chopped coriander.

# Escalopes Cooked on a Hot Stone

*Sukha Gosht*

This dish is traditionally made with lamb, but I use it for escalopes of veal or turkey breast. If a cooking stone is not available, a griddle will do equally well. It is very good food for slimmers.

6 meat escalopes (scallops) beaten flat
6 cloves garlic
3cm / 1¼ inch piece fresh root ginger
15ml / 1 tbsp freshly ground black pepper
10ml / 2 tsp ground cumin
10ml / 2 tsp ground cardamom
10ml / 2 tsp ground cinnamon
2 fresh hot green chilli peppers, seeded
60ml / 4 tbsp lemon juice
5ml / 1 tsp salt
15ml / 1 tbsp vegetable oil

In a food processor, make a paste from all the ingredients except the meat and vegetable oil. Rub paste into the meat and leave it to marinate for at least 4 hours. Heat the cooking stone or griddle, oil it very lightly and cook the escalopes for a few minutes on each side.

# Lucknow Leg of Lamb
### *Mussallam Raan*

Lucknow became important when Moghul Delhi was collapsing and the
Nawabs of Oudh were notorious for their extravagant lifestyle and lavish feasts.
This recipe was perfected by one of their legendary cooks. These cooks were
highly prized and they kept their secrets in the family. The Nizam of Hyderabad
and the Maharajah of Jaipur persuaded the Nawab to 'loan' them cooks who were
close relatives and one of their descendants, Mohmmad Islam, still cooks this dish
in the Jaipur Rambagh Palace Hotel.

1 leg of lamb, weighing 2kg / 4½lb
8 whole green cardamom pods
10 cloves
15ml / 1 tbsp black peppercorns
30ml / 2 tbsp white poppy seeds
4 dried hot red chilli peppers
500ml / 16fl oz plain yoghurt
30ml / 2 tbsp vegetable oil
2 large onions

6 cloves garlic
4cm / 1½ inch piece fresh root ginger
15ml / 1 tbsp paprika
10ml / 2 tsp grated nutmeg
10ml / 2 tsp ground mace
10ml / 2 tsp ground cinnamon
15ml / 1 tbsp salt
30ml / 23 tbsp slivered almonds

Grind all the whole spices and mix with the yoghurt. Heat the oil and fry the
finely chopped onions, garlic and ginger until they are golden brown. Work in a
food processor to a paste with all the other ingredients except the lamb and
almonds. Remove the skin and membranes from the lamb and prick all over,
right down to the bone. Rub the paste all over the lamb, pushing it into the holes.
Leave to marinate overnight in the refrigerator.
Roast the paste-coated lamb in a 180°C / 350°F / gas 4 oven, turning it from time
to time and basting it with the juices in the roasting tin. Scatter the slivered
almonds over the meat when it is cooked and brown in the oven or under a hot
grill (broiler).

# Lamb Biryani
## *Shah Jahani Biriyani*

The Great Moghuls descended from Genghis Khan and Tamburlaine, but by the time they seized power in India in the sixteenth century they had developed a taste for fine living. Barbour created beautiful water gardens and poetry; music and literature delighted his court. Food became very elaborate and many contemporary miniatures show the emperors being served elegant dishes. For them, these lovely lamb and rice dishes were lavishly decorated with costly fruit and nuts. This was Shah Jahan's favourite.

800g / 1¾lb boned lean lamb, cubed
3 whole green cardamom pods
2cm / ¾ inch piece cinnamon stick
3 cloves
15ml / 1 tbsp white poppy seeds
10ml / 2 tsp ground cumin
5ml / 1 tsp ground mace
1 medium onion
3cm / 1¼ inch piece fresh root ginger
4 cloves garlic
2 fresh hot green chilli peppers
30ml / 2 tbsp ground almonds
10ml / 2 tsp salt
30ml / 2 tbsp vegetable oil
200ml / 7fl oz plain yoghurt

*Rice*

300g / 10oz (1⅔ cups) basmati or long-grain rice
4 whole green cardamom pods
2cm / ¾ inch piece cinnamon stick
5ml / 1 tsp rose water
10ml / 2 tsp salt
600ml / 1 pint (2½ cups) water
5ml / 1 tsp saffron threads
15ml / 1 tbsp warm milk
200ml / 7fl oz cream

*Garnish*

20ml / 1½ tbsp slivered almonds
20ml / 1 ½ tbsp halved cashew nuts
15ml / 1 tbsp halved, skinned pistachio nuts
30ml / 2 tbsp sultanas (golden raisins)
silver *vark*, if available

Grind the whole spices for the meat mixture and work to a paste in a food processor with the other spices, the onion, ginger, garlic, chilli peppers, ground almonds, salt and a little water. Heat the oil and fry the spice paste until the oil starts to separate out. During this period you must stir all the time. Stir in the cubes of lamb so that they are coated with the sauce. Add about 100ml / 3½fl oz water, cover and simmer gently until the meat is almost done. Now beat the yoghurt with a little water and stir into the mixture. Reduce to a thick sauce.

Meanwhile, cook the rice with the spices, rose water, salt and water in a heavy-based tightly covered pan. Boil for 15 minutes, then leave undisturbed off the heat for another 10 minutes. Dissolve the saffron in the warm milk and stir into the cream.

Choose a deep oven dish with a tight-fitting lid and grease lightly. Arrange half the rice at the bottom and pour over half the cream mixture. Arrange the meat on top in an even layer, then cover with the remaining rice and pour over the last of the cream mixture. The lid can either be sealed on with a flour and water paste or the dish covered first with foil, crimped tightly around the edges, and then the lid. Cook in a preheated oven at 150°C / 300°F / gas 2 for about 45 minutes. To serve, turn out on to a large dish and decorate with the lightly roasted or fried nuts, sultanas (raisins) and *vark*.

# Parsi Lamb with Straw Potatoes
## *Sali Ma Gosht*

This Parsi recipe was cooked for me in Delhi by Mrs. Bhicoo Maneckshaw, a whirlwind of energy and enthusiasm, who has written cookery books, planned VIP menus for Indian Airlines and taught Indira Ghandhi's daughters-in-law to cook.

**800g / 1¾lb boned lean lamb from the leg, cubed**
**500g / 1lb 2oz potatoes**
**salt**
**45ml / 3 tbsp vegetable oil**
**2 large onions**
**4 cloves**
**4cm / 1½ inch piece cinnamon stick**
**5 whole green cardamom pods**
**7.5ml / 1½ tsp turmeric**
**7.5ml / 1½ tsp ground cumin**
**4 cloves garlic**
**3cm / 1¼ inch piece fresh root ginger**
**oil for deep frying**

Cut the peeled potatoes into very thin sticks and rinse in several changes of cold water. Put the potatoes in a bowl of salted ice-cold water and chill in the refrigerator while you cook the meat.

Heat the oil and cook the sliced onions with the cloves, cinnamon and cardamom pods until the onions are brown. Now add 5ml / 2 tsp water with the turmeric, cumin and finely chopped garlic and ginger. Simmer for 5 minutes, adding a little more water if the mixture seems too dry. Now stir in the meat pieces with 250 / 8fl oz water and salt to taste. Cover and cook until the meat is tender. Only a thick sauce should remain.

To make the straw potatoes, take a handful at a time, squeeze well and dry in a tea (dish) towel. Deep fry, using a skewer to keep the straws separate. Drain on kitchen paper.

Turn the meat on to a serving dish and top with the crisp straw potatoes.

# Eggs and Cheese

Although eggs do not play an important role in Indian cooking, the Parsis have some interesting recipes. Vegetarians who eat eggs can substitute hard-boiled eggs for meat in many of the recipes. Cubes or bâtons of Indian cheese can be added to many of the vegetable dishes to make them more nourishing.

# Indian Cheese
## *Paneer*

Paneer is the mainstay of the majority of Indian vegetarians and it is used in a myriad of ways. It cannot really be replaced by ricotta or cottage cheese because paneer keeps its consistency when it is cooked. However, paneer is very easily made so this presents no problems.

**2 litres/3½ pints (2 quarts) milk**
**60ml / 4 tbsp lemon juice**

Heat the milk, stirring occasionally to avoid a skin forming. When it comes to the boil, stir in the lemon juice and remove from the heat. The milk will curdle instantly. Pour it through a strainer lined with fine muslin or cheesecloth, placed over a bowl, and leave for at least an hour so that the whey drains out.
To make a block of paneer, put the soft curd, still wrapped in the muslin or cheesecloth, in a press or on a plate under a very heavy weight. Leave for several hours. When it is really firm it can be cut into cubes or sticks.
The cheese will keep for 48 hours in the refrigerator.

# Cheese Balls Covered with Potatoes & Peas

*Paneer Alu Mattar Patties*

200g / 7oz *paneer*, ricotta or cottage cheese
350g / 12oz boiled potatoes
500g / 1lb 2oz (3 cups) shelled peas
15ml / 1 tbsp vegetable oil
2 cloves garlic
3cm / 1¼ inch piece fresh root ginger
5ml / 1 tsp turmeric
5ml / 1 tsp cayenne pepper
salt
4 fresh hot green chilli peppers
100g / 3½oz (1 cup) dry breadcrumbs (optional)
oil for deep frying

**Batter**
100g / 3½oz (1 cup) chickpea flour, (besan)
250ml / 8fl oz water
salt

Heat the vegetable oil and fry the finely chopped garlic and ginger until golden brown. When cold, mix with the mashed cheese and roll into small balls. Leave in the refrigerator for at least 20 minutes. Cook the peas with a little salt and the chopped, seeded green chilli peppers; drain and make into a coarse purée. Make sure that the pea purée is quite dry. Enclose the cheese balls with a coating of pea. Dip in the batter, then roll in breadcrumbs and deep fry. Drain on kitchen paper. Process the boiled potatoes with the turmeric and cayenne pepper to make a smooth paste. Form into small patties and carefully enclose the cheese balls. Return to the refrigerator to chill for 10 minutes. Make sure that the pea purée is quite dry and enclose the potato balls with a coating of peas. Dip in the batter then roll in breadcrumbs and deep fry
Serve hot, whole or cut in half to show the different layers.

# Indian Cheese with Mushrooms & Peas

*Mattar Paneer*

This is a mild but tasty vegetable side dish.

100g / 3½ oz *paneer*
250g / 9oz mushrooms
250g / 9oz (1⅔ cups) shelled fresh peas
50g / 2oz (4 tbsp) *ghee* or butter
5ml / 1 tsp cayenne pepper
5ml / 1 tsp turmeric
15ml / 1 tbsp chopped fresh coriander leaves
salt

Melt the *ghee* and add the peas and sliced mushrooms. Cook for a few minutes, then stir in the spices, chopped coriander, salt to taste and the cheese cut into cubes. Simmer for about 5 minutes, cover and keep warm until ready to serve.

# Cheese in Spicy Sauce
### *Paneer Makhani*

This dish was created for vegetarians but it can be enjoyed by all of us. For this recipe it is not possible to use a ricotta or cottage cheese in place of *paneer*.

250g / 9oz *paneer* (see page 92)
oil for deep frying
50ml / 2fl oz plain yoghurt
15ml / 1 tbsp vegetable oil
2 medium onions
5ml / 1 tsp ground cumin
5ml / 1 tsp ground coriander
5ml / 1 tsp turmeric
5ml / 1 tsp *garam masala*
10ml / 2 tsp cayenne pepper
salt
300g / 10oz (1½ cups) peeled, chopped tomatoes
150ml / 5fl oz cream
15ml / 1 tbsp chopped fresh coriander leaves

Heat oil and deep fry the *paneer*, cut into bâtons or sticks, until it is golden brown. Drain on kitchen paper, then put on a plate and pour over the yoghurt. Heat the vegetable oil and fry the finely chopped onions until they are soft. Stir in the ground spices and, after a few minutes, the tomatoes with salt to taste. Add a little water if the sauce seems dry and simmer for 10 minutes. Add the cream and heat gently. Now spoon in the *paneer* together with the yoghurt and, before serving, sprinkle with fresh coriander.

# Parsi Scrambled Eggs
## *Akuri*

A delectable Parsi egg dish, ideal for a simple lunch or supper

> 6 eggs
> 50g / 2oz / 4 tbsp butter
> 2 small onions
> 2cm / ¾ inch piece fresh root ginger
> 2 fresh hot green chilli peppers
> 30ml / 2 tbsp peeled chopped tomato
> 30ml / 2 tbsp chopped fresh coriander leaves
> 5ml / 1 tsp turmeric
> 60ml / 4 tbsp milk
> 5ml / 1 tsp salt
> 2.5ml / ½ tsp black pepper

Heat the butter and cook the finely chopped onions,
ginger and chilli peppers until they are soft. Add
the tomato, chopped coriander and turmeric.
Beat the eggs with the milk, salt and pepper
and stir into the mixture in the pan. Cook
until the eggs are a creamy consistency.
Serve hot with Indian bread or toast.

# Rice

*I*n India, rice is the single most important crop and today takes up one-quarter of the cultivated land. In the South and East it is the essential part of every meal and, even in regions where traditionally wheat bread takes precedence, rice is still consumed in huge quantities. In religious ceremonies it is used to symbolise plenty and fertility, and the western custom of throwing rice at weddings undoubtedly has the same significance.

The best rice is the basmati rice grown around Dehra Dum in the foothills of the Himalayas. This fragrant rice improves with age and is usually carefully matured. Basmati rice needs to be rinsed in several changes of water to remove the loose starch and then soaked for an hour before cooking. This makes the rice white and increases its absorbency, but the grains are fragile and must never be stirred too roughly. Other long-grain rices are cheaper, less delicate and require no soaking, but for special dishes basmati is worth the time and expense because good basmati rice has an unmistakable perfume.

In the West, we are often rather intimidated by our reputation for producing soggy rice, but this can be avoided if the basic rules are followed: Measure the volume of rice before it is rinsed. The drained rice should then be cooked in a heavy saucepan with a close-fitting lid, covered by twice its volume of water. Allow 7.5–10ml / 1½–2 tsp salt for every 500g / 1lb 2oz (3 cups) rice. Cook for about 20 minutes. The most important moment is the 'resting' period after the rice is cooked: it must be left undisturbed in its covered saucepan for at least 5 minutes so that the grains remain separate and intact. If you omit this step the rice will become mushy and the texture of the dish will be spoiled.

### Plain boiled Basmati rice

Measure rice allowing 350g / 12oz (2 cups) of basmati rice for 6 people. Rinse well in cold water to remove excess starch.

Soak in cold water for 1 hour.

Cook in twice volume of water, 750ml / 1¼ pints (3 cups) in a saucepan with a tight-fitting lid, adding 20ml / 4 tsp salt

Bring to the boil and cook for 20 minutes. Remove from heat. Do not remove lid, but allow to rest for another 5–10 minutes.

# Lemon Pullao with Cashew Nuts
## *Nimbu Kaju Pullao*

This delicious lemon rice is very simple to prepare yet adds a sumptuous touch to any meal. I find it a godsend when entertaining since the recipe calls for cooked rice. I prepare everything in advance, concentrate on the other dishes, and at the last minute stir the cooked rice into the waiting pan of spiced lemon juice.

150g / 5oz (1 cup) long-grain rice
100g / 3½ tbsp (⅔ cup) roasted cashew nuts
60ml / 4 tbsp yellow split peas (*channa dal*)
15ml / 1 tbsp white gram beans (*urad dal*)
50ml / 3½ tbsp vegetable oil
5ml / 1 tsp black mustard seeds

2 fresh hot green chilli peppers
15ml / 1 tbsp chopped fresh root
 ginger
5ml / 1 tsp turmeric
60ml / 4 tbsp lemon juice
8 fresh or dried curry leaves
salt

Cook the rice, then drain and set aside. Wash the *dal* then put to soak in cold water to cover for several hours. Drain and dry on kitchen paper. Heat the oil, add the *dal* and cook, stirring, until they begin to change colour. Scatter in the mustard seeds and when they begin to pop, add the seeded and finely chopped chilli peppers and ginger. Cook for a few minutes, then add the turmeric, lemon juice and curry leaves. When the mixture begins to bubble, stir in the rice. Check for seasoning and add salt if necessary. Cover and cook gently until the rice is heated through, adding a little more water if the rice seems too dry. Add half the cashew nuts, broken into pieces, and fluff up the rice with a fork. Turn on to a heated serving plate and sprinkle the remaining nuts on top.

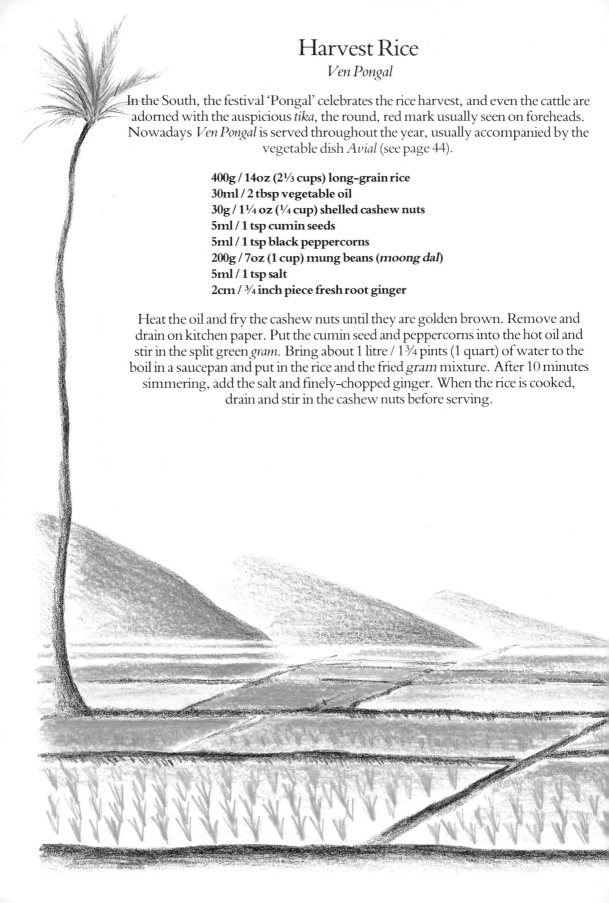

# Harvest Rice
## *Ven Pongal*

In the South, the festival 'Pongal' celebrates the rice harvest, and even the cattle are adorned with the auspicious *tika*, the round, red mark usually seen on foreheads. Nowadays *Ven Pongal* is served throughout the year, usually accompanied by the vegetable dish *Avial* (see page 44).

**400g / 14oz (2⅓ cups) long-grain rice**
**30ml / 2 tbsp vegetable oil**
**30g / 1¼ oz (¼ cup) shelled cashew nuts**
**5ml / 1 tsp cumin seeds**
**5ml / 1 tsp black peppercorns**
**200g / 7oz (1 cup) mung beans (*moong dal*)**
**5ml / 1 tsp salt**
**2cm / ¾ inch piece fresh root ginger**

Heat the oil and fry the cashew nuts until they are golden brown. Remove and drain on kitchen paper. Put the cumin seed and peppercorns into the hot oil and stir in the split green *gram*. Bring about 1 litre / 1¾ pints (1 quart) of water to the boil in a saucepan and put in the rice and the fried *gram* mixture. After 10 minutes simmering, add the salt and finely-chopped ginger. When the rice is cooked, drain and stir in the cashew nuts before serving.

# Rice with Morels
## *Gochian Pullao*

This is a Kashmiri recipe which uses the fragrant local black mushrooms.

400g / 14oz (2½ cups) long-grain rice
200g / 7oz fresh morels or 25g / 1oz dried
60ml / 4 tbsp vegetable oil
2 large onions
5ml / 1 tsp cumin seeds
1 bay leaf
3 cloves garlic
5 cloves
10ml / 2 tsp salt
5 whole green cardamom pods
5cm / 2 inch piece cinnamon stick

If you are using dried morels, they should be soaked for at least an hour in warm water, then rinsed in several changes of water. Fresh morels should be wiped clean and cut in half.

Heat the oil and fry one of the onions, finely-sliced, until it is a deep brown and quite crisp. Drain on kitchen paper and reserve to crumble over the dish just before serving.

Put the cumin seeds in the oil and when they begin to spatter, add the second onion, finely-chopped with the garlic. Now add the mushrooms, spices, bay leaf and salt and stir for 5 minutes. Stir in the rice until each grain is coated with oil. When the rice begins to change colour, pour in 1 litre/1¾ pints (1 quart) of boiling water. Stir well and cook with the lid half on for about 15 minutes. Now cover tightly and, on a very low heat, cook for another 10 minutes. At the end of this time, turn off the heat but leave undisturbed for 15 minutes.

Remove the lid, fluff up with a fork and transfer to a serving dish. If you wish you may omit the topping of crisp fried onions.

# Yoghurt Rice
## *Masuru Anna*

This rice dish is found all over the South, but I first discovered it in Mysore in a small local restaurant where the food is served on banana leaves. The bearer sets the leaves on the table in front of each customer and then pours a small quantity of water over the leaf. The customer runs his hand over the leaf to remove the surface water and the various dishes, vegetarian or non-vegetarian, are then ladled on to the leaves. The food is eaten by hand, without spoons or forks.

150g / 5oz (1 cup) long-grain rice
400ml / 14fl oz plain yoghurt
10ml / 2 tsp salt
15ml / 1 tbsp vegetable oil
5ml / 1 tsp black mustard seeds
6 fresh or dried curry leaves
2 cloves garlic
2cm / ¾ inch piece fresh root ginger
3 fresh hot green chilli peppers
30ml / 2 tbsp chopped fresh coriander leaves

Cook the rice in salted water until it is tender. Drain and stir the yoghurt into the hot rice. Heat the oil and add the mustard seeds. When they begin to pop, add the curry leaves. When they start to curl, pour the oil over the rice. Stir in the finely chopped garlic, ginger and seeded chilli pepper and the fresh coriander.

# Mint Pullao
*Pudina Ka Pullao*

This is a rice dish with great flavour. I must confess I have sometimes made it with cooked rice and it has still tasted good.

350g / 12oz (2 cups) basmati or long-grain rice
50g / 2oz (1 cup) fresh mint leaves
50g / 2oz (½ cup) freshly grated coconut
2 fresh hot green chilli peppers
2.5ml / ½ tsp ground cloves
2.5ml / ½ tsp ground cinnamon
15ml / 1 tbsp vegetable oil
20ml / 4 tsp salt

Wash the rice under cold running water and leave to soak in water to cover for an hour. Work the coconut, seeded chilli peppers, mint and spices in a food processor, adding about 75ml / 5 tbsp water to make a smooth paste. Heat the oil and gently fry the mint paste until the fat begins to separate out. Stir in the drained rice so that every grain is coated with the paste. Now pour in 750ml / 1 ¼⅜ pints (3 cups) boiling water and add the salt. Cover the pan and cook gently for 15 to 20 minutes, until the water is absorbed. Leave covered in the pan until ready to serve.

# Yellow Spring Rice
*Peeley Chaawal*

In February, all over India, the coming of Spring is celebrated with the Vasant Panchami festival. It is usual to wear yellow clothes and cook yellow food. This rice is good enough to be eaten all through the year.

300g / 10oz (1¾ cups) basmati or long-grain rice
50g / 2oz (4 tbsp) butter or *ghee*
3 cloves
4 cloves garlic
2 medium onions
5ml / 1 tsp turmeric
10ml / 2 tsp salt
1 bay leaf
15ml / 1 tbsp vegetable oil

Wash the rice under the cold running water and leave to soak in water to cover for an hour. Heat the butter and put in the cloves. When they begin to swell add the finely chopped garlic and one of the onions, also finely chopped. When the onions begin to soften stir in the turmeric and the drained rice. Add salt, the bay leaf and 600ml / 1 pint (2½ cups) water. Cover tightly and cook over a low heat until the rice is tender and all the liquid is adsorbed. The rice will keep warm for some time in the covered saucepan.
Slice the remaining onion into fine rings and cook in the heated oil until deep brown and crisp. Crumble over the rice just before serving.

# Bread

*I*n north and central India, families turn simple meals into feasts with their fragrant hot bread called *roti*. The bread is usually unleavened and the most common flour used is whole wheat. Most Indian families make the bread daily by hand. These bread doughs can be quickly prepared and I usually use my food processor. Any heavy iron frying pan or griddle can be used to replace the traditional, slightly concave *tava*. Although the dough does not need to rise it should be left in a warm place for about half an hour before rolling out. However, the whole process is much quicker than making western-type bread. If you want, the dough can be made the previous day and left in the refrigerator overnight. It will then need an hour in a warm room before rolling out.

I love *naan* straight from a real *tandoor* oven, but because homemade versions seem disappointing, I cook other breads at home.

# Flat Griddle Bread
## *Chappati*

The humble chappati, the staple bread eaten by all the people of India, assumed a rather sinister significance in 1857 when the Great Mutiny, now known as The First War of Independence, was heralded by the mysterious Chappati Movement. Chappatis were passed by hand from village to village, sometimes covering a distance of 325 kilometres in a single night. Even those handing on the chappatis did not know the precise meaning, but a general feeling of unrest and impending doom was quickly created. Today all is forgotten, and chappatis are happily passed around the table with no dire consequences.

**225g / 8oz (2 cups) white chappati flour or whole wheat flour**
**2.5ml / ½ tsp salt**
**175ml / 16oz water**

Sift the flour and salt into a mixing bowl or food processor (discard the bran) and gradually work in enough water to make a firm dough. Knead very thoroughly, then leave the dough to rest in an oiled plastic bag for an hour or so. If preferred the dough can be prepared the day before. Divide the dough into four or six balls and roll each out to form a flat disc about 3mm / ⅛ inch thick. Leave to rest for about half an hour, covered with a damp cloth. Heat a griddle without any fat until it is very hot, then proceed to cook the first chappati. The edges of the chappati should be pressed down very firmly against the cooking surface so that bubbles are formed in the bread. When brown spots begin to appear turn over to cook the other side. The cooked chappatis are then often held by tongs over a medium naked flame until they bubble and swell up, but this stage can be omitted. If you intend to make a larger quantity, the cooked chappatis can be stacked, wrapped in foil and kept in a warm place until ready to serve. Cold chappatis tend to be rather leathery and unappetizing.
Makes 4 or 6.

# Bread Stuffed with Spiced Potatoes
*Aloo Paratha*

These breads, eaten with a little yoghurt salad, can make a delicious but simple supper.

400g / 14oz (3½ cups) whole wheat flour
salt
120g / 4oz (1 stick) butter
water to mix
oil and butter for cooking

**Filling**
175g / 6oz potatoes
1 fresh hot green chilli pepper
2cm / ¾ inch piece fresh root ginger
20g / ⅔oz (½ cup) fresh coriander
  leaves
2.5ml / ½ tsp cayenne pepper
salt

To make the filling, boil the potatoes in their skins. Drain well, then peel and mash them. Remove the seeds from the chilli pepper and chop finely with the peeled ginger and the fresh coriander. Mix together with the potato and season with the cayenne pepper and salt to taste.
In a food processor, mix the flour, salt and butter together and add a little water, about 15ml / 1 tbsp, just enough to make a firm dough. Divide into 12 balls and put aside, covered with a damp cloth.
On a lightly floured surface, roll out two of the balls to flat discs of about 10cm / 4 inches in diameter. Place a little of the filling on one disc and cover it with the second disc. Use the rolling pin to gently flatten the bread and seal the edges. The bread will now be about 17.5cm / 7 inches in diameter. Heat the *tawa*, or griddle, brush with oil and cook the bread, turning it once. Traditionally, the bread is only half cooked on the griddle. Then a little butter is melted in a non-stick pan and the *paratha* are shallow-fried to a crisp finish; however, the frying can be omitted and all the cooking done on the griddle. Continue to make the remaining breads in the same way, keeping them warm in the oven. When all are cooked, serve them hot.
Makes 6.

# Potato Cakes
## *Aloo Roti*

This homely bread is simple to make, and served with a bowl of soup it makes a satisfying lunch or supper.

**4 large potatoes**
**150g / 5oz (1¼ cups) whole wheat flour**
**5ml / 1 tsp salt**
**3 fresh hot green chilli peppers**
**45ml / 3 tbsp chopped fresh coriander leaves**
**40g / 1½ oz (3 tbsp) butter**
**vegetable oil for frying (optional)**

Boil the potatoes in their skins, drain well and peel. Work in a food processor with the flour, salt, seeded and chopped chilli peppers, coriander and melted butter to make a soft dough. Be careful not to over-process to the point of the dough becoming a paste that sticks to the processor bowl. Leave in a warm place for about half an hour. Divide into six portions and roll out each to form a disc about 15cm / 6 inches in diameter. These breads can either be cooked on an oiled heavy griddle or lightly fried until each side is nicely brown.
Makes 6.

# Punjabi Corn Bread
## *Makki Ki Roti*

This simply prepared bread comes from the Punjab. The dough is more easily made by hand, becoming a little too tough in the food processor.

**400g / 14oz (3¼ cups) corn meal**
**salt**
**175ml / 6fl oz boiling water**
**melted butter**

Put the corn meal and salt in a bowl and make a well in the centre. Pour in the boiling water and mix with a spatula to make a stiff dough. Divide it into 12 balls, rest for 30 minutes and roll each out to a disc about 3mm / ⅛ inch thick, and 10cm / 4 inches in diameter. Cook until brown on both sides on a lightly oiled griddle or heavy pan. Spread a little melted butter on each bread and stack them on a heat-proof plate. Keep warm in the oven until all the breads are cooked, then serve with more melted butter.
Many interesting variations can be made with this basic bread mix, by adding cumin seeds, garam masala, chopped fresh coriander or other spices.
Makes 12.

Put corn meal and salt in a bowl.

Add boiling water and mix to a stiff dough.

Divide into 12 balls, rest for 30 minutes, then roll out.

Cook on a lightly oiled griddle, and flatten with spatula.

Turn to brown on both sides. Stack and serve hot with more butter.

# Fried Puffed Bread
## *Poori*

These spectacular puff balls are served all over central and southern India, and they are quick and easy to make. Although they can be cooked in advance and kept warm, they inevitably deflate, so I only prepare them when I know I can make a batch to be eaten immediately by family and friends.

**250g / 9oz (2¼ cups) fine white chappati flour or whole wheat flour**
**2.5ml / ½ tsp salt**
**about 250ml / 8fl oz water**
**vegetable oil for deep frying**

Sift the flour and salt into a mixing bowl or food processor (discard the bran) and work in enough water to make a dough. Knead well, then cover with a damp cloth and let the dough rest for at least half an hour. When just about ready to eat, divide and knead the dough into 10 smooth, small balls. Take one ball, leaving the others covered, and knead again, then flatten it slightly between your hands. Brush each side with a little vegetable oil, and using a rolling pin, roll out to a thin disc 6 to 8cm / 2½ to 3 inches in diameter.
Heat vegetable oil in a deep pan or wok until very hot, and then cook the pooris one at a time over a moderate heat. When the poori is put in to the hot oil it will float and you must keep pressing it down with a slotted spoon until it swells and puffs up. Then turn it over and do the same with the other side. The whole process only takes about 30 seconds. The golden balls should be drained on kitchen paper, then served as soon as possible. Makes 10.

# Whole Wheat Rolls
## *Batti*

Batti used to be the Rajput warriors' iron rations in desert skirmishes. The bread was buried in the hot sand in carefully marked locations and if supplies did not arrive the men cracked open the hard bread and poured in nourishing *ghee* to make a one-dish meal. Today, this Rajasthani speciality is usually cooked in hot ashes and the dust is brushed off before serving. I only make this bread when I have an open wood fire, but I confess I wrap each ball of dough in foil before putting it in the hot ashes to cook. They can also be baked in a moderate oven.

**500g / 1lb 2oz (4½ cups) whole wheat flour**
**5ml / 1 tsp baking powder**
**5ml / 1 tsp salt**
**80g / 3oz (5 tbsp) *ghee* or melted butter**

Sift the flour, baking powder and salt into a large bowl (discard the bran) and gradually mix in about 300ml / 10fl oz water to make a firm dough. Leave to rest, covered, for about 10 minutes. Gradually work in the fat and knead to form a soft dough. Leave, covered, for about 20 minutes, then divide into 16 balls. Leave these to rest for at least half an hour, or until you are ready to bake them, in hot ashes or a 180°C / 350°F / gas 4 oven, for 20 minutes. Makes 16.

# Poori

Sift flour and salt in bowl or processor.

Work in enough water to make a dough.

Divide into 10 balls and knead until smooth.

Knead and then roll out one ball at a time.

Cook one at a time and push down until bread puffs up.

After a few seconds, turn over.

Drain and put on kitchen towel paper.

Serve hot immediately.

# Chutneys, Pickles & Raitas

$M$ost Indian families take pride in their homemade pickles and chutneys, and it is considered rather shameful to serve any variety bought in a shop. Houses are adorned with rows of jars maturing in the sun on the windowsill, and a hostess is often judged by the number of relishes she serves. I must confess I usually serve 'bought' mango chutney, decanted into a small bowl, but I do make one of these simple relishes to serve in another bowl.

The refreshing *raitas* are a 'cool' element to be served with the main meal, the spicy chutneys add interest to bland menus. Both are to help with the balance and general elegance of the total effect.

# Coriander, Mint & Yoghurt Chutney
*Dhania Podina Chutney*

This chutney is very easily made and goes very well with most kebabs.

**100g / 3½ oz (2 cups) fresh coriander leaves**
**40g / 1½ oz (¾ cup) fresh mint leaves**
**100ml / 3½fl oz plain yoghurt**
**20g / ⅔oz (2 tbsp) onion**
**1cm / ½ inch piece fresh root ginger**
**2 fresh hot green chilli peppers**
**5ml / 1 tsp sugar**
**5ml / 1 tsp salt**

Chop the onion and the peeled ginger and place them in a food processor. Add the seeded chilli peppers with the rest of the ingredients. Process to make a smooth sauce.

# Walnut Chutney
*Akhrote Chutney*

Kashmir gives us this easily-made walnut chutney which goes very well with most meat and vegetable kebabs.

**100g / 3½oz (1 cup) shelled walnuts**
**120ml / 4oz plain yoghurt**
**15ml / 1 tsp cayenne pepper**
**salt**

Put all the ingredients into a food processor and work to make a smooth paste. If you prefer a 'cooler' chutney, cut down the quantity of cayenne pepper.

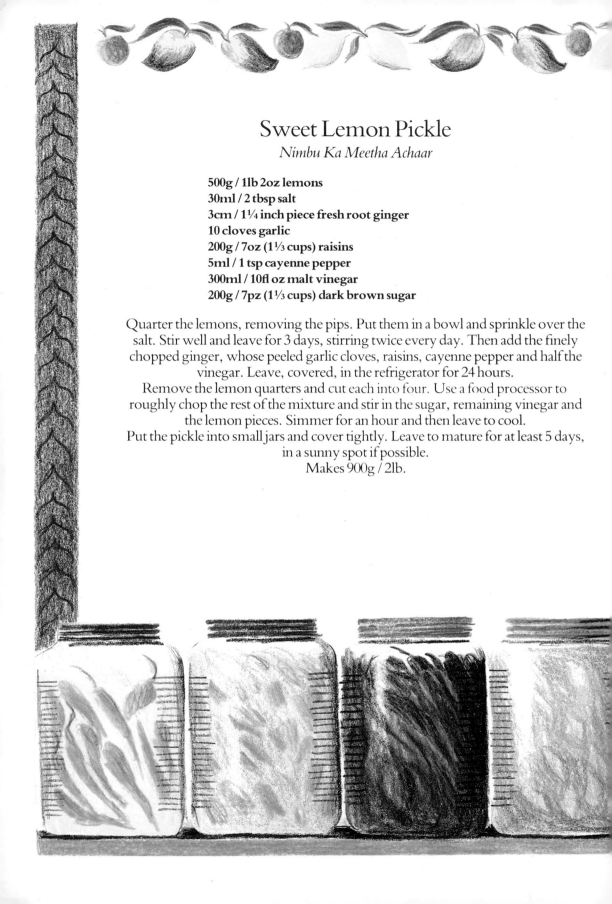

# Sweet Lemon Pickle
### *Nimbu Ka Meetha Achaar*

**500g / 1lb 2oz lemons**
**30ml / 2 tbsp salt**
**3cm / 1¼ inch piece fresh root ginger**
**10 cloves garlic**
**200g / 7oz (1⅓ cups) raisins**
**5ml / 1 tsp cayenne pepper**
**300ml / 10fl oz malt vinegar**
**200g / 7pz (1⅓ cups) dark brown sugar**

Quarter the lemons, removing the pips. Put them in a bowl and sprinkle over the salt. Stir well and leave for 3 days, stirring twice every day. Then add the finely chopped ginger, whose peeled garlic cloves, raisins, cayenne pepper and half the vinegar. Leave, covered, in the refrigerator for 24 hours.
Remove the lemon quarters and cut each into four. Use a food processor to roughly chop the rest of the mixture and stir in the sugar, remaining vinegar and the lemon pieces. Simmer for an hour and then leave to cool.
Put the pickle into small jars and cover tightly. Leave to mature for at least 5 days, in a sunny spot if possible.
Makes 900g / 2lb.

# Mint Chutney
### *Pudina Ki Chatni*

**100g / 3½oz (2 cups) fresh mint leaves**
**1 small onion**
**2 cloves garlic**
**1 fresh hot green chilli pepper**
**15ml / 1 tbsp lemon juice**
**5ml / 1 tsp salt**
**5ml / 1 tsp cayenne pepper**
**100ml / 3½fl oz water**

Process all the ingredients to make a thick paste (seed the chilli pepper first if you prefer a milder chutney). Pour into a small bowl and keep, covered, in the refrigerator. Coriander chutney can be made by substituting fresh coriander for mint.

# Cucumber Raita

*Khira Raita*

**1 large cucumber**
**10ml / 2 tsp salt**
**2 spring onions (scallions)**
**1 fresh hot green chilli pepper, seeded**
**300ml / 10fl oz plain yoghurt**
**15ml / 1 tbsp lemon juice**
**5ml / 1 tsp ground cumin**
**30ml / 2 tbsp chopped fresh mint leaves**

Dice or shred the cucumber, sprinkle with 5ml / 1 tsp salt and leave for an hour. Rinse and pat dry. Put the other ingredients, except the mint, into a blender, work to a purée and pour this liquid over the cucumber. Turn into a serving bowl and keep cool. At the last minute, stir in some of the mint and sprinkle the rest on top.

# Spinach Raita

*Palak Raita*

**500g / 1lb 2oz fresh spinach leaves**
**5ml / 1 tsp salt**
**500ml / 16fl oz plain yoghurt**
**2.5ml / ½ tsp freshly ground black pepper**
**1 fresh hot green chilli pepper**
**2.5ml / ½ tsp cayenne pepper**

Rinse the spinach and cook very quickly in a saucepan until wilted, with just the moisture remaining on the leaves and a little salt. Immediately plunge the spinach into cold water to preserve the bright green colour. Drain well, then chop finely and stir in the yoghurt, black pepper and seeded chilli cut into very fine rings. Turn into a serving bowl and, just before serving, sprinkle with the cayenne pepper.

# Desserts

*I*n India sweet things have a religious significance, and honey, milk, sugar, *ghee* and water are regarded as the food of the gods. Most desserts contain these ingredients with the addition of fried fruits and nuts. They are offered to friends as a sign of love and affection, and they are often served, at the beginning of a meal as a prayer, rather in the same way as some Westerners say 'grace'. At weddings the very auspicious sweet *laapsi* is served and the bridal couple personally hand it to each guest. Some of these recipes do not work with pasteurised milk and they are nearly all too sweet for my taste. Even in India many families rely on professionals for sweets, and the Bengali sweet-makers are considered the tops. For this reason I have chosen three desserts which always please. I usually serve these or tropical fresh fruit at the end of an Indian meal.

# Yoghurt & Saffron Cream

*Shrikhand*

This delicate, pale yellow dessert from Western India is very easily made, and health–conscious cooks can use low-fat yoghurt. However, I find it works best with thick, full-fat yoghurt.

800ml / 1⅓ pints (3¼ cups) plain yoghurt
5ml / 1 tsp saffron threads soaked in 20ml / 4 tsp warm milk
5g / 3oz (6 tbsp) sugar
2.5ml / ½ tsp ground cardamom
5 shelled pistachio nuts

Line a sieve with muslin or cheesecloth and put in the yoghurt to drain for about 8 hours in a cool place. Put the drained yoghurt in a food processor with the sugar and process for a few minutes. Fold in the ground cardamom and saffron mixture. Spoon the cream into individual bowls and decorate with the peeled and slivered pistachio nuts. Chill before serving.
For international cooks, a variation of this traditional recipe can be served by folding in:

500g freshly sliced peaches or
500g fresh raspberries

Fold together at the last moment and serve.

# Perfumed Ground Rice

*Phirni*

This dessert is found all over India, and it is usually served in small, unglazed pottery bowls, called '*shikoras*', which absorb the moisture and help the dessert to set.

175g / 6oz (1 cup) ground rice
1 litre / 1¾ pints (1 quart) milk
200g / 7oz (1 cup) sugar
5ml / 1 tsp rose water
5ml / 1 tsp ground green cardamom seeds
30ml / 2 tbsp slivered almonds
15ml / 1 tbsp raisins
5ml / 1 tsp peeled, slivered pistachio nuts

Mix the ground rice to a smooth paste with 225ml / 7½fl oz water. Bring the milk to the boil and stir in the rice. Simmer for 10 minutes, stirring continuously. Add the sugar, rose water, cardamom, almonds and raisins. Pour the mixture into small bowls and decorate with pistachios. Serve very cold.

# Mango Mousse
*Aam mousse*

In India, the most prized fruit is the Alphonso mango. Indira Gandhi's passion for these was notorious, and Nehru always contrived to keep her supplied even when she was imprisoned during the Second World War or on her honeymoon in Kashmir. They are the most versatile fruit and appear in many guises. London's 'Bombay Brasserie' restaurant serves delicious Mango Bellinis (champagne poured on to fresh mango juice) as an aperitif, and I feel they make the perfect end to the meal. I often make a mango mousse or ice-cream.

**1 large, ripe mango**
**30ml / 2 tbsp lemon juice**
**1 sachet (11g / 0.4oz) powdered gelatine**
**(or 2 envelopes unflavoured gelatin)**

**30ml / 2 tbsp sugar**
**200ml / 7fl oz double (heavy) cream**
**2 egg whites**

Add 30ml / 2 tbsp hot water to the lemon juice, and dissolve the gelatine in this. Allow to cool. Peel and stone the mango and process to a smooth purée with the sugar. Stir in the gelatine. Leave in the refrigerator for about 15 minutes while whipping the cream and beating the egg whites until they are stiff. Fold the cream and egg whites into the mango mixture. Spoon into individual bowls, or pour into an ornamental mould. Leave it to set in the refrigerator before serving, or turning out.

# Index

RICKSHAW                    LUDWIG